Sharks Don't Sink

Sharks Don't Sink

Adventures of a Rogue Shark Scientist

Jasmin Graham

with Makeba Rasin

PANTHEON BOOKS

NEW YORK

All rights reserved. Published in the United States by Pantheon Books, a division of Penguin Random House LLC, New York, and distributed in Canada by Penguin Random House Canada Limited, Toronto.

Pantheon Books and colophon are registered trademarks of Penguin Random House LLC.

Page 211 constitutes an extension of this copyright page.

Library of Congress Cataloging-in-Publication Data
Names: Graham, Jasmin, author. | Rasin, Makeba, author.
Title: Sharks don't sink : adventures of a rogue shark
scientist / Jasmin Graham, with Makeba Rasin.
Description: First edition. | New York : Pantheon Books, [2024]
Identifiers: LCCN 2023050534 (print) | LCCN 2023050535 (ebook) |
ISBN 9780593685259 (hardcover) | ISBN 9780593685266 (ebook)
Subjects: LCSH: Graham, Jasmin. | Women marine biologists—
United States—Biography. | African American scientists—
United States—Biography. | Sharks—Research.
Classification: LCC QH91.3.G73 A3 2024 (print) |
LCC QH91.3.G73 (ebook) | DDC 597.3092 [B]—dc23/eng/20231213
LC record available at https://lccn.loc.gov/2023050534
LC ebook record available at https://lccn.loc.gov/2023050535

www.pantheonbooks.com

Jacket photographs: (top) by Cassie Wegeng; (middle)
by Julia Wester, courtesy of the Field School; (bottom)
by Jackson Coles, courtesy of the Field School
Jacket design by Perry De La Vega

Printed in the United States of America

First Edition

2 4 6 8 9 7 5 3

To my family, both those who are living and those who have passed on. I am truly standing on the shoulders of giants. But I do not stand alone, so I also dedicate this book to all the people (and animals) who have supported me, both personally and professionally, on this journey.

Sharks Don't Sink

Prologue

My life was changed forever by a single photograph. It was of a Black female researcher floating underwater with an adorable nurse shark. Nurse sharks are large coastal sharks that like warm waters, like those of southern Florida. Nurse sharks are like cats: they have "whiskers"—extensions on their lips called barbels—and they are cute and seem cuddly when they want to be, but when they don't want to, boy, they're ready to fight you. I love how fun it can be to just vibe in the ocean with them when they're happy with you.

In the photo, I could see the sunlight refracted through the clear turquoise water and thick, familiar seagrass dancing at the scientist's feet. It looked like many of the places where I work, a natural cathedral of bending light and amazing creatures. I laughed when I saw that the researcher was wearing all pink and red: pink bathing suit, red rash guard, popping pink nail polish—even her snorkel was Barbie pink.

I sat up straight with my phone in hand. It was after midnight. I was still awake after most of my neighborhood had turned in—except, of course, for the perpetual salsa party

3

One of the photos posted on Twitter, under #BlackInNature, of researcher Carlee Jackson Bohannon conducting a snorkel survey on nurse sharks in Belize

up the street. Even my dog, Iggy, was fast asleep in his crate, upside down like a dead bug. I'd been scrolling on Twitter when I came across the scientist's post, #BlackInNature. *What?!* I thought. *A Black* woman *working with sharks! There's more than just me?*

I'm a marine biologist and shark scientist; at the time, I was the only Black member of the American Elasmobranch Society (AES), a professional scientific society for those who study sharks, skates, and rays: fish with cartilage skeletons rather than bones. I was in the midst of writing a paper on a large-scale study that synthesized data from members of the Smalltooth Sawfish Recovery Implementation Team, which is in charge of stewarding the conservation efforts of this charismatic and critically endangered animal. Lately, though, I'd been telling myself that when this paper was published, I was done with science. *Get me outta here!* I loved doing

4

science, but I also loved my mental health, and the two just didn't seem compatible anymore. I was on the verge of giving up a career in a field that I was passionate about because I was burned out and didn't have the energy to keep fighting for space any longer.

In another photo, the same woman scientist was leaning over the side of a boat, her hand affectionately resting in front of a lemon shark's dorsal fin and her red nails gleaming in the bright sun. Her hair was natural, like I wear my hair when out in the field, and her excitement was palpable, the way I still feel no matter how many times I'm around these majestic animals. Sharks are truly the most amazing creatures you could ever meet—they can do things no other animals can; they can adapt to changes in their environment in ways that no other animal can; and they have survived longer than many other animals in the course of natural history. R.E.S.P.E.C.T. These creatures are one of a kind. Dinosaurs don't have nothin' on sharks for resilience and ecological importance.

Looking at these photos, I wondered: Could there be a world in which I didn't have to give up studying these amazing creatures?

"Yay for Black girls who study sharks. We should start a club lol," I tweeted at this mystery woman, hoping she could feel my smile.

I was still staring at her photos when she tweeted back.

"I am so so serious we should," she wrote. Her name was Carlee Jackson Bohannon, and I learned that she was a shark conservationist and marine-turtle specialist working in South Florida, not far from where I lived. The tweets flowed for a

Carlee Jackson Bohannon conducting
a shark survey in Florida

bit, and then Amani Webber-Schultz and Jaida Elcock, two other shark scientists, entered the conversation. Here were two more Black women in what I thought was the small world of shark science. I felt like I had discovered a unicorn—and then another and then another. We moved over to DMs and in a flurry of excitement, each of us explained how we knew from an early age that we wanted to work on the water—that it was what we felt we were meant to do.

Jaida grew up landlocked in the desert in Arizona. She always knew she wanted to work with animals in some way, and after a high school internship at an aquarium in Scottsdale, she became hooked on sharks. Now she is a PhD stu-

dent at the MIT–Woods Hole Oceanographic Institute Joint
Program. Amani grew up in the San Francisco Bay area and
had the Pacific Ocean and the Monterey Bay Aquarium as
her backyard. In high school, she took part in a coral reef
restoration project in Fiji, which got her interested in conservation. While studying marine sciences as an undergrad, she
won a scholarship that allowed her to do fieldwork studying
sharks, and there she discovered that being out on a boat
and working up—catching, gathering scientific data from,
and then releasing—sharks brought her more joy than she'd
ever experienced before. She is now getting her PhD at the
New Jersey Institute of Technology. Meanwhile, Carlee was
raised in Detroit, Michigan, without any access to the ocean.
When she was about five or six, she picked up a book about
sharks and fell in love. From that point on, she decided she
was destined to become a shark scientist, and ended up with
undergraduate and graduate degrees in marine biology. After
listening to these amazing stories, I told all of them about my
own childhood, growing up as a military brat and living all
over the country, but falling in love with the ocean on visits
to my grandparents in South Carolina.

Even those of us who grew up landlocked or without
access to the ocean had found our way to the sea, and we all
marveled that we got to do this work—*who knew this was
a job?* But we also all had stories, one eerily similar to the
next, of daily, casual racial microaggressions (and sometimes
macroaggressions) from peers who seemed to have no clue
how internalized their bias was or that our differences could
actually be an asset. We swapped stories about often being
left to clean up after a meeting or being spoken to as if we

were lazy (not one of us is lazy). All of us seemed united by our feelings of exclusion but also by our mutual passion for sharks, and I felt the warmth of belonging for the first time in a long, lonely while.

Just a few months before we met, I had burned out completely. My nerves had been ground into dust by trying to succeed alone as a unicorn in a horse-dominated world that hated horns, a.k.a. academia. Until this point, science had always been a refuge and a source of fun for me. But now it had morphed into something far less positive, and I tumbled into hopelessness. When my hair began to fall out, I knew I had to do something to get better. Sometimes, you *don't* got this, and you need to take care of yourself. If it's between saving the sawfish and saving myself, there's really no choice.

What killed me was I knew this wasn't just a *me* problem. I had the work ethic, the skills, the curiosity, and a growing list of credentials that would be the envy of any scientist. It was more a *them* problem—a toxic, white, male-dominated publish-or-perish environment laced with so much casual and overt sexism and racism that people didn't even seem to notice it because it was seen as "just the way it is." I had always known, since I was a kid, that I didn't have to take other people's BS, that I deserved better, but it was hard to let go of my dreams of being a professor at one of the many Historically Black College and Universities (HBCUs) with my own lab.

It nearly crushed me, but I did it: I left academia. I left Tallahassee as I was wrapping up my master's from Florida State University, and moved to the Tampa Bay area, where my mentor, Tonya Wiley, was based. I rested. I recuperated. And I reflected on what might be next.

Then, in the spring of 2020, the pandemic hit, and the rest of the world pressed Pause, just like I had. It was during the height of lockdown, with the Black Lives Matter movement taking off, that I came across Carlee's post and the beautiful photos of her working with sharks.

#BlackInNature was created after a Black man named Chris Cooper was threatened by a white woman while he was birdwatching in New York City's Central Park. Like so many during those isolating months of pandemic shutdown, Cooper, an avid birder, was enjoying spending time outside. He knew that dogs were supposed to be kept on a leash in that section of the park so that they wouldn't scare off the wildlife, and so he asked a woman politely to leash her dog. The woman flew into a rage. She called 911, explaining to the dispatcher that she was being threatened by a Black man and begging for the police to come and rescue her, which was a false accusation and a particularly dangerous one during a brutal season of wrongful death—without recourse—of Black citizens by the police. Watching the video Cooper made of the interaction, you can tell the woman *knew* that her comfort was worth more than his life. She felt secure enough to yell for help, safe in the knowledge that the cavalry would come, no questions asked. But, as a Black man in America, Cooper had no such safety. The incident took place on the same day that George Floyd was murdered by a police officer in Minnesota, and it was in the wake of several extrajudicial killings in 2020, such as that of Breonna Taylor, asleep in her home, and Ahmaud Arbery, killed while out for a jog. (We can only imagine how many more such killings occurred but didn't trend on social media.) These were the events that led to the summer of national and global Black Lives Matter protests.

This was the world in which #BlackInNature flourished on Twitter, inviting me and other Black folks to share in our pleasure of being outdoors—birding, jogging, or anything else—while being Black. I loved seeing the bountiful Black joy popping up in my feed. People on the water, in the mountains, in the woods—unworried, unhurried—just vibing. It was beautiful, an antidote to the horror accumulating in all our feeds.

A white shark scientist also replied to Carlee and me on the Twitter chain and then DM'd me to let me know that she had a research vessel docked in Miami and she would be more than happy to provide us with accommodations for us to meet up, if we were serious. I had no idea who this person with the outsized generosity was, but Amani and Carlee knew her to be someone who supported women in science whenever she could. Her name was Dr. Catherine Macdonald, and, at the time, she was the founder and director of a Miami-based nonprofit called the Field School, which was devoted to creating inclusive environments for young marine scientists to learn and conduct research out on the water. She wrote, "100 percent serious on our end. We're all yours." In time, I'd come to learn that Catherine has an inner compass I truly respect: she says and then *does* what she means.

Trips on a field boat, where scientists fish for sharks, collect data, and put tags on the animals, are often inaccessible to young students of color because of the cost of travel and the fact that you have to pay your way onto a boat if you're not already in a research program. So Amani, Carlee, Jaida, and I decided to take Catherine up on her offer and meet in Miami, but to also make the meeting an all-expenses-paid opportunity for younger shark scientists of color to join us and learn. If Catherine and the Field School were providing everything once we got to Miami, we just needed to fundraise enough to get people there. Catherine offered to let us do that through the Field School, and earmark donations for our group. So all we needed was a name. We landed on Minorities in Shark Sciences, because we wanted an easy acronym (MISS) that alluded to us being started by women but was inclusive of all who identified as a gender minority.

Call it a cosmic alignment, call it divine intervention, call it whatever you want, but the creation of MISS was special. Two weeks after our Twitter meet-cute, on Juneteenth, 2020, the four of us unicorn sisters launched MISS. Money poured in through the website Amani put together. Via many small donations, we quickly reached our goal of $12,000, and then passed $25,000, which meant the workshop wouldn't be a one-off; we would be able to do more in future years. MISS seemed to take on a life of its own: people kept sending in money, but also notes of gratitude and encouragement for a science space that was accessible and inclusive. A tsunami of emails crashed into our inboxes from people of color around the world looking to us to make a wave of change in the shark world. Could we help them find labs that were inclusive? Could we help introduce them to scientists and build their professional networks? Could we help them find paid research experiences? We weren't surprised that, if all of us felt alone in our work and studies, many other people felt isolated, too. But we were surprised by how many of us were out there, scattered, looking for one another. When we all found one another, my hope and excitement for my own future was rekindled.

.   .   .

Just as we Black women scientists have struggled to thrive in our field, sharks have struggled to survive, too. In the last century, some shark populations have decreased by as much as 90 percent. While sharks have a super-bad reputation in popular media—consistently portrayed as scary, bloodthirsty, mindless killing machines—the truth is that it's sharks that are under threat. On average, only ten people a year are killed by shark encounters. Most of the time, when people have encounters with sharks, they need a Band-Aid, maybe a stitch or two, because sharks usually bite humans just to figure out what the heck they are (they don't have hands, so they have to feel with their mouths)—not to kill. Meanwhile, according to a 2013 paper in *Marine Policy,* an average of one hundred million sharks a year die from encounters *with people.* In an encounter between a shark and a person, it's the shark that, more often than not, is going to end up dead. I've pulled sharks out of the water that have gunshot wounds; I've seen videos on the internet of people putting harnesses on sharks and dragging them behind boats, beating them with clubs, and otherwise brutalizing them.

While it's true that sharks are so powerful that even an

exploratory bite can mean a human might end up maimed or worse, it's only in extremely rare cases that an individual dies or loses a limb—a rarity that makes such stories seem "newsworthy" and more likely to spread, feeding into the myth that humans are prey for sharks. If a beachgoer has an encounter with, say, a leopard shark—which is an adorable creature that's generally passive and friendly toward humans—the local paper will use a photo of a teeth-baring

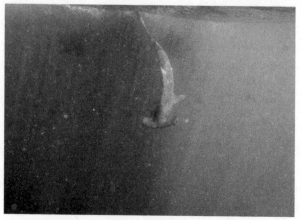

Underwater footage of a great hammerhead
happily swimming off after being released from
a shark workup at our MISS workshop

great white shark for maximum effect. There's an amazing amount of diversity within the shark superorder, and many of the creatures are small and kinda silly. Just look at these cutie-pies.

But you don't see these kinds of images in the wider media.

Sadly, a bad reputation isn't the only challenge sharks face. Overfishing and habitat loss are hard on all fish, but it is particularly hard on sharks because of the way they reproduce.

Amani Webber-Schultz and Jaida Elcock
bringing a baby nurse shark on board the
research vessel *Garvin* for a workup

Many sharks have only a few pups a year. Those pups may take twenty years to mature, which means they will not be able to bounce back from overfishing as fast as salmon, for example, which have many babies and a shorter life cycle. Sharks, in scientific terms, are what are called K-selected animals. R-selected species have evolved to grow really fast, reproduce a lot, and then die quickly, like those salmon. K-selected ones have evolved to grow really big, be really efficient, live a long time, but have fewer babies, like sharks. One strategy isn't better than the other. They're just different goals—spread like grass (R-selected seeds) or grow big for hundreds of years like sequoia trees (K-selected seeds). But it is really hard to be evolved for K-selection and then switch. We don't suddenly have elephants (K-selected animals) that start having the lifespan of mosquitoes (R-selected). Once evolution has driven you in a direction, you're kind of stuck.

And unfortunately, a lot of these K-selected species that were doing fine are struggling now. Trees, coral, sharks—all of which require a lot of time and energy to develop into highly efficient or complex organisms—aren't able to recover at a rate faster than we humans are removing them from the environment.

This is a crisis, one that was preventable and now urgently needs to be fixed. Over millions and millions of years, sharks have changed only slightly; they hit on a near-perfect form from the earliest phases of their evolution and, unlike some mammals or reptiles, have needed only small adjustments over the millennia, but never an overhaul of their entire system. For example, in the hundreds of millions of years that sharks have been around, the *T. rex* no longer exists, and its closest relative is now the chicken. But if you look at a shark swimming off the coast of Florida today, it's more or less the same as a shark in the time of the dinosaurs.

In terms of their sheer ability to survive, sharks are incredible. They have a cartilaginous vertebra, which makes them light and fast for their size, and which has aided in their resilience. If a bony fish was the size of a shark, it would be much heavier and inflexible. Although they don't have a swim bladder to help them stay afloat, like many bony fish, sharks have large pectoral fins and oily livers that are less dense than seawater, which prevents them from sinking to the bottom of the ocean. Sharks have the same five senses we have, though much keener, plus a sixth sense: amazingly, they can sense electrical charges, so that even when a prey or predator is almost entirely invisible to them, they can still sense the electrical impulse that the other creature's heart creates as it beats.

In addition to being so wonderfully built, sharks have an incredible diversity of adaptations. Some sharks can swim in salt water and switch into brackish or fresh water—their bodies actually have the ability to adapt to the change in salinity of the water. While some sharks need to keep moving in order to breathe, called ram ventilation, others have an adaptation that means they are able to be still and push water over their gills to take in oxygen, referred to as buccal pumping.

Yet even though sharks are practically perfectly adapted to their role and environments as marine predators in so many ways, they still need our protection, because perfection doesn't actually matter in nature. Luck plays a huge part in survival—an often-overlooked aspect of evolution and science. Sharks are ideally adapted to marine life, but after surviving all known mass extinctions, thanks to natural selection and diversity, they now find themselves deeply unlucky. More than a quarter of the world's shark species are now threatened by extinction.

So I don't just love sharks, I feel for them. I admire their persistence, their resilience, their ability to survive, to keep moving forward; but I'm also laser-focused on their vulnerabilities, their need for our protection. I see myself and my people in sharks. All too often Black people are perceived and treated much like sharks: feared, misunderstood, and brutalized, often without recourse; assumed to be threatening when so often we're the ones under threat; portrayed unfairly in the media, so that others are predisposed to have a negative interaction with us. It's very hard to imagine a white person being shot at point-blank range after being pulled over by a cop for a simple traffic stop, or being throttled to death for selling cigarettes on a street corner. If it did happen, there would be a national outcry and rules would be put in place to make sure it never happened again. But not for Black people. And in the same way, try to imagine folks going around dragging dolphins behind boats or beating turtles to death. You can't. People would be up in arms if that happened. Campaigns to save the dolphins and turtles would be everywhere. But not for sharks.

The reality is that sharks are essential. These prehistoric animals help maintain balance in an ecosystem by weeding out the weak and sick fish and by controlling the movements of their prey. And if an ecosystem collapses, life in our oceans dies, and so, eventually, do we. Our strength as humans lies in our amazing diversity within our own species and those around us—and we ignore this truth at our peril.

As scientists, we recognize the importance of biodiversity; however, for some reason many people in the field struggle to see that we need diversity not only in nature, but in research and experience. That is how we get true diversity of thought. In the same way that different animals bring different skills and ecosystem functions to create a harmonious environment, so, too, do different people with different backgrounds and lived experiences bring those skills to any scientific endeavor.

· · ·

MISS was created to help protect the diversity in the oceans *and* the diversity within the marine science field. Its founding also brought me back from the brink. Connecting with Carlee, Amani, and Jaida, first online and then in the real world, helped me begin to imagine another path for myself. Maybe I could find a new way to practice science that would mean I could protect my mental health *and* the marine life I loved so much. Maybe I could help protect my fellow unicorn sisters, this family I had found, as well.

After MISS formed, I finally moved on from burnout—and from quitting science altogether. I became what I call a "rogue scientist." I decided I would practice science independently, without any academic affiliation or institution. Could I make this work? I didn't know for sure, but I knew I had to try.

This book is the story of that first experimental field season going rogue, in the summer of 2022. With MISS already up and running for about a year, I was now doing science again, hustling for funding and boat time, working outside of academia, with this amazing community of people by my side. It's about what happens when someone sidesteps the system—a system that isn't made for them and doesn't value them—to create another way. It's also the story of my journey to become a shark scientist as a young Black woman from a family rooted in the South, whose members have fought for our right to exist peacefully for centuries. And, importantly, it's a celebration of sharks—all they can teach us about how to live, how to survive and thrive, and how it's up to us now to help them continue to swim, lest we all sink.

1

Field Season 2022
Day One on Research Vessel Garvin
Biscayne Bay, Florida

The calm marina waters in Biscayne Bay lap against the bow of the boat, and for a moment, a deep calm settles over me. The seabirds swoop over nervous water—water that is flat and smooth, then suddenly ripples because a predator is chasing a school of small fish. The deck is my favorite spot on the *Garvin,* a large research boat run by the Field School. I hug my knees into my chest and let the blazing Florida sun warm my face. Being on the water is my church, where I come to get quiet and take a breather. There is so much going on in these shallow coastal waters that it helps put my relentless worries into perspective—the water may look placid, but it is full of life and mystery. I'm but a small piece in this big world.

I see a tarpon rolling in the distance, its shiny scales sparkling like a million diamonds. I love watching them roll, because they're a marvel, so big and strong yet nimble: like a linebacker doing ballet or a whale breaching the water—there's just a whole lot of *stuff* to throw up into the air. There's a sheepshead under the dock and those strange fish always make me laugh out loud: stripes like a zebra and big, straight teeth like a middle-aged dentist. I sit, taking it all in. The big plexiglass platform on the *Garvin* where we work up large sharks sparkles in the sunshine. High overhead the wind flaps the boat's flags: the Stars and Stripes, Black Lives Matter, and a Pride flag. The *Garvin* is the biggest research vessel I have ever been on, a four-star hotel compared to the more common motel-like skiffs—and it is also the only research vessel I have ever been on whose flags announce to everyone that all are equal, all are welcome, and all belong on this boat.

The research vessel *Garvin* during a MISS workshop

I could sit here until dusk, watching the water, letting time pass, and enjoying the wide, open space, but not today. I have things to do. I'm ready to begin again, to succeed despite *them.* My bare feet pad across the rough deck, my heart lurching because I'm so excited for our team to start collecting data for a study on hammerheads both here in Biscayne Bay, on the Atlantic coast of Florida, and in Tampa

Bay, over on the Gulf side. This is my first research project since leaving academia to work as a rogue scientist, without an affiliation to an institution. Going forward, I'm committed to contributing to peer-reviewed, quality publications, and doing research in a**hole-free spaces, only.

I walk around to do a visual check of the gear: longlines, gangions, bait, drumlines, yo-yos, floats, rope, tags, scissors, extra cryovials to collect samples, the lactate machine (which measures the stress in sharks' blood), the board we will use when we take photos of hammerheads, some extra biopsy punches to collect muscle tissue, and a few acoustic transmitters (which track animal movements), just in case we catch a sawfish. I am first and foremost a sawfish researcher (more on that later), but hammerheads were my first love, and I am excited to return to them.

Finally, I check the items for the swag bags that we give to workshop participants. They have tons of cool stuff, like matching leggings donated by Waterlust and International Sawfish Day stickers. This weekend I'm running a MISS workshop for emerging scientists who identify as Black, Indigenous, and/or people of color (BIPOC) and are interested in marine field research. In the last two years, students have started to come to us seeking what they cannot get in academia: safety, access, a sense of belonging, and mentorship. I feel tears suddenly, and it takes me by surprise: I want everything to be perfect for these young students.

In the salon, which is like the living room on the boat, I grab some venison jerky I brought for the group snack pile, and await the arrival of Jaida, who is flying down from Cape Cod. Field School director Dr. Catherine Macdonald has left bedsheets neatly folded on the couch, so I grab them and start making up everyone's beds. There will be twelve of us staying on board—the four MISS co-founders, two MISS members serving as guest instructors, and six student participants. Each berth is very small, and the mattresses on the bunk beds are an irregular size, so putting on the fitted sheets turns out to be a minor battle. I put my sleeping bag in the berth by the stairs, my favorite bed on this boat.

Biscayne Bay is a nursery to many animals, including several shark and ray species, my area of focus; but it sits right next to Miami, a huge metropolitan area that runs way up the coast with very few natural (and necessary) barriers. On an undisturbed coast, the natural progression would be ocean, sand dunes, grass, marsh, forest, and so on to protect the water from the land, and vice versa. Some coastal cities— like Charleston, South Carolina, where I went to college— are better than others at keeping or maintaining natural barriers, like dunes, but Miami hardly has any. There's often just a boardwalk or a parking lot right up to the water. And so, especially when it rains, tons of trash flows straight into Biscayne Bay from the city. Fertilizer from the golf courses, oil from cars, and anything else that gets washed down the drains goes smack into the bay. Nutrients like nitrogen and ammonia, which occur naturally in the bay, are present in excess. Biscayne Bay is about as humanly impacted as a body of water can be while still supporting a lot of life. This makes it a perfect place to study how people affect shark and ray communities.

It's a little like choosing among your children, but my favorite sharks are called bonnetheads. They are one of the smallest members of the hammerhead family. As the name implies, they have little, shovel-like heads that resemble bonnets. Bonnetheads are nervous balls of stress. Just like some people are more prone to anxiety than others—me; I'm some people—some animal species are more prone to stress, for different biological and physical reasons, such as brain chemistry and structure. Having struggled with anxiety since childhood, I know it doesn't feel good. When we start pulling sharks out of the water tomorrow, the first and last thing we will do is take a blood sample and compare stress-hormone levels before and after, to determine how difficult the encounter was for them. I love these silly little fish. When people think "shark," they often imagine ferocious and angry monsters, but these guys usually max out at just over one meter and are kinda comical. They wouldn't harm anybody.

I've worked with bonnetheads in Tampa Bay and areas along the Gulf Coast of Florida as well as the Florida Keys, and yet I have never seen ones that look like those in Biscayne Bay. Last year, in 2021, when I went out on the *Garvin* for the first time with Catherine, a teeny, tiny male bonnethead came up on our longline, and I wrote "immature" on the data sheet, because there was no way that minuscule thing was an adult. But, as we handled it, we found it had claspers, the male reproductive organ, and the claspers were calcified (not bendable) and so it had to be an adult male bonnethead. I erased "immature" and wrote "mature," but I couldn't believe it. How was this possible? Bonnetheads are typically small but not this small.

Furthermore, in Tampa Bay, where I live and usually fish with my primary fishing partner, Tonya Wiley, we've only ever caught bonnetheads in a gill net, which we use when trying to catch smaller fish.

"Do you guys catch a lot of bonnetheads on a longline?" I asked Catherine.

"Yeah, loads," she said.

I was gob-smacked: they looked different and they behaved differently.

I went home and reviewed the literature on hammerheads in these waters, and there was nothing about the size difference. I just kept thinking about them. The bonnetheads in Biscayne were just *weird:* smaller than any others I had seen, like the tiny yet mature male, and very light in color, with more freckles than usual. And they took a baited hook! Tonya had never seen that before in over a decade of working with these guys. This may mean nothing at all, but it shows a significant difference in behavior or eating strategy. So I must know: Why? What is driving even this small change in behavior? How does it affect the survivability of the bonnets here? Maybe the difference is insignificant, or maybe it is a small piece of information to help us understand the larger chain of interconnection between bonnethead behavior and their environment.

I emailed Catherine a few weeks after that outing to see if it would be possible to do research in Biscayne Bay on the *Garvin,* comparing the hammerheads there to the ones in Tampa Bay. She was totally down, and said she had an advisee, Kathy Liu, a MISS member at the University of Miami, whom she'd love for me to work with, if I was open to it. I love a win-win; I was thrilled to have the help.

Our plan is to use a variety of techniques to better understand the differences between the hammerheads in these locations, and explore possible factors that could be driving the differences: Is it the environment and the water quality in Biscayne Bay that is impacting their growth and development? Is it what they eat, and is there a shortage of food for these animals? Or perhaps they are actually a new, distinct, cryptic species—animals that look the same but are in fact genetically different. There could be major conservation and management implications if it turns out the bonnethead population is lower than we realized. It would be dope to discover a new species, but this seems the more unlikely outcome. No matter what the data reveal, we will be able to provide new information about members of the hammerhead family, many of which are vulnerable.

But so what? you might say. Well, sharks are very, very old. We estimate they've been around for four hundred to six hundred million years. (And even that large variance is because scientists can't agree on what counts as a true shark!) They're older than most things. They're older than trees, than the rings of Saturn. They were here before dinosaurs. It's been a long time since this planet has known an ocean without sharks. We have no way to understand what the ocean would be like without them and what the direct or indirect domino effects would be if we removed them. And for the first time in recorded history, we're losing them at an alarming rate.

For example, when my parents or grandparents were my age, sharks were in abundance in these Florida coastal waters and the Gulf of Mexico. Marine biologists in my parents' youth would not have been nearly as concerned about the scarcity of sharks. Unlike today, when we tag them and release them back into the water, researchers would have regularly kept them for samples, so unworried were they about the ability of these ancient fish populations to survive. The rich waters around Florida were filled with snook, mahi-mahi, king mackerel, bonnetheads, scalloped hammerheads, weird and wild-looking sawfish, and a rich and exciting mix of other fish. But in the last century, some shark populations have seen brutal declines. Scalloped hammerheads, for example, are estimated to have declined by over 75 percent in one fifteen-year period, according to a large-scale study of shark populations in the North Atlantic. That rate is almost unfathomable. And because we do not yet understand the exact impacts—especially for weirdos with weird heads (like hammerheads), which may serve a specific function in the ecosystem—their loss could be more harmful than we realize.

Extinctions are, of course, a part of life; they are common and happen all the time. However, evolutionary extinction happens over millions of years, unless there is an extreme event like an asteroid or a super volcano. Let me repeat that: *species go extinct over millions of years,* not thousands and certainly not hundreds, as we are seeing currently. Shark populations are being decimated faster than they can recover. Sharks have survived all five known mass extinctions, including the most recent one sixty-five million years ago that ended the dinosaurs. But if things continue as they are, many of them may not make it through the looming sixth extinction: the Anthropocene extinction, also known as the human-created extinction. So basically, humans are as destructive as an asteroid or super volcano (not a great look for mankind). We are simply killing sharks faster than they can reproduce.

Much research in shark and ray science and conservation is around the idea that if we can better understand sharks—the way they look, their evolution, their nutrition, their behavior, the ways they move and travel, their reproduction, and so on—we can work to better protect them. And while popular perception seems to think that sharks are killing machines and some may even think "good riddance," nothing could be further from the truth. We need them. Predators help create a healthy ecosystem by maintaining balance and diversity. Without them, all life—including that of humans—is threatened.

And weirdos like hammerheads can teach us a lot, because they offer us so many questions. Like: there are sharks that have been around for four hundred fifty million years and look basically the same as one another, and then you have these other ones with wild, bizarre heads. *What's going on there? What does this head do?* Despite all the interest and curiosity and wonder they elicit, no one has any idea (though there are some unconfirmed theories, such as the head allowing for an increased field of vision or better steering, or being used to pin down stingrays while hunting). A common understanding of evolution would have us think this unique head must have a purpose; if it has been passed down again and again, it must be important, right? So what invaluable role does it play? These animals are vulnerable, and if their unknown value in supporting or regulating an ecosystem disappears, what would happen to marine life? I'm excited to try to figure it out. Though I do wish I didn't have to wonder how much longer these sharks will be around for us to study at all.

. . .

I fell in love with the water as a child, fishing with my dad. My mother was a nurse in the air force, and we moved around a lot—Alabama, California, and Texas, before finally settling in South Carolina. In a childhood of changes, new places, new friends, new houses, and new schools, the one constant was our summers and vacations in Myrtle Beach, South Carolina. My dad's family are all very close, and in the otherwise very white city of Myrtle Beach, they started out in a Black neighborhood the locals called Harlem and then moved to another Black neighborhood affectionately called the Hill, just a stone's throw from the water. My grandmother Evelina's house wasn't much to look at, but it was the center of my family. It had a yard, some grass but no trees, and a small driveway. On the porch she had white plastic chairs, and the front door was always open, so you could see through the clear plastic storm door and out into the neighborhood. One block over from my grandmother's house is my aunt Carol's house; halfway down the street on the opposite side is my aunt Rose's house. Keep going to the end of that street and my aunt Ernestine's house is on the corner, right on a big main road. Aunt Ernestine used to have a gorgeous view of the ocean, a billion-dollar view—literally. But developers built high rises, a convention center, and a Sheraton between her and the ocean, and she can't see anything now but the fronts of buildings, places she could never afford to live.

Many of the families in those small houses in Harlem have been on this patch of land for a long time. My great-grandfather Luther Graham Sr. bought land there in 1942. Like all newly free Black people, my family never got the promised forty acres and a mule, but Luther was able to buy

My grandma Evelina's house in Myrtle
Beach, South Carolina, on the Hill

a small plot of land in the area they had inhabited for as far back as we can trace. The land that is now Myrtle Beach sits between the ocean to the east and the intercoastal waterway to the west; the soil is sandy. European settlers had tried to raise crops there, like tobacco and indigo, but without much success, and it was uninhabited for a long while. But my family planted what they could and, like the Waccamaw people had done before there were Europeans or Africans trying to make a life here, they fished and were able to feed themselves.

Fast-forward to when the thinking among white people changed from "Oh, I want farmland and therefore this crap isn't for me" to "Oh, I want beachfront property, and there is only so much, so we want this land now." In the 1920s, white developers began building resorts and making this small stretch of beach a vacation destination to rival those in Florida. The city was incorporated in 1938, and, like most of the American South—but not just the South—it was for white people only. The segregated beaches excluded Black people and enforced this exclusion with legal or extra-legal violence. If a Black person went to a white beach, they risked being imprisoned, or worse.

And so a Black developer bought land just north of Myrtle, which became Atlantic Beach, also known as the Black Pearl. This was where Black people could go to the beach, and it may even be the only Black-owned beach in the country today. But, alas, my family was already in Myrtle Beach, where they had always lived. So the Myrtle Beach of today—the hotels and seaside resorts—built itself around the Grahams. Despite Klan intimidation, Jim Crow segregation, rising property taxes, gentrification, and the city's attempts to use eminent domain to move us over the years, my family has remained in the Hill. The city has managed to shrink the neighborhood, but the small, run-down houses across the street from world-class resorts are still there. It's our home.

Even though the Hill sits right next to the water, my dad's family hardly ever go there to hang out or relax because the beach was still segregated up until my aunt Rose graduated from high school in 1966 or 1967 and family habits get passed down through generations. My parents grew up during the civil rights era, when protesters in the South were doing sit-ins at lunch counters, but also marching onto segregated beaches in places like South Carolina, Florida, and Mississippi, staging what were known as "wade-ins," where they'd walk into the ocean despite the police being there to beat them back. On August 30, 1960, a group of civil rights activists organized a wade-in at Myrtle Beach State Park, but the park officials blocked and arrested them; they drove them to the county line to be chased out by a white mob. By the time I came to Myrtle Beach, the beach was legally integrated, but not a place of comfort. We found comfort elsewhere when I was a little kid: all those decades of white supremacy and racial terror meant that we instinctively stayed away from the beach.

Thankfully, we always found a place to fish. For Christmas the year I was six, my parents and I drove up to Myrtle Beach from where we were stationed in Texas, a place known as Tornado Alley. (That was our least favorite station by far.) Everyone in my family fishes—but my dad especially loves to fish. And, as a child, I loved to do whatever my dad was doing. I went everywhere with him; people called me his shadow. He had a seat for me on his bicycle back at the base, and he'd go about his business, doing whatever he did, taking me along. When he realized I liked things that he liked, it was the best: he was so proud. My first fishing pole was a yellow Tweety Bird rod that he bought for me, and which he still has to this day.

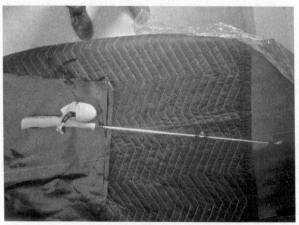

My very first fishing rod, which my
father has kept to this day

When I picked out a fishing hat for him for Father's Day, he wore it proudly. It read MY FISH above a picture of a teeny, tiny mullet, and MY KID'S FISH above a picture of a huge flounder. I got a good laugh out of that hat.

In Myrtle Beach, Dad and I fished off the Springmaid pier. It had no signage and the wood was weathered; you could get a splinter in the summertime if you weren't careful. But that Christmas I particularly remember, it was cool and breezy, and I wore sneakers. Year-round it smelled like fish, sea salt, and cigarettes, specifically Black & Milds.

Most of the fishermen on the pier recognized my dad from the neighborhood. They were set up for the day: coolers and chairs set out, rods in the holders and lines in the water already, some of them probably there since sunup.

"Hey, Sidney," someone said.

"Hey, man," my dad said.

"How ya doing?"

"Every day above ground is a good day," my dad replied.

These were people who lived to fish. Even on workdays, they would head out to the pier the minute they clocked out. They came for the recreation, because fishing made them happy, but also because they could eat what they caught, sharing it with their families and their community.

The pier was high and long. All or almost all the people on the beach were white, staying at the hotels, and everyone on the pier was Black and from the Hill. There was probably a public access point to the beach from it, but it wasn't obvious, and remember: going to the beach wasn't something my family or the folks from the Hill did.

Dad put down the cooler and his little tackle box and

leaned our rods against the railing. I watched as he unfolded our chairs. My grandma had packed us sandwiches, and I nibbled while he baited the hooks—I didn't learn to rig a fishing line until I was about ten or eleven. He used night crawlers and blood worms for bait because they were the easiest to come by; most gas stations in Myrtle Beach carried them.

There was some Kool-Aid and water for me in the cooler, and two Cokes for my dad. Daddy had two or three left-handed rods with him since he's kind of left-handed. He does almost everything right-handed, but he fishes left-handed because he learned to fish with a left-handed rod. Everyone else was right-handed and the left-handed rod was the one not in use. I am naturally right-handed, but since Daddy taught me to fish, I fish with my left hand, too. When I am out on the *Garvin* or field boats, someone will notice that I haul in a line and wrap the yo-yo with my left hand instead of my right.

"Jasmin," they ask, "are you left-handed?!"

"Well, kind of," I reply.

Dad cast out; he was trying for spot. For me, we were hoping for maybe some croaker: fish that don't require technique, just bait. My dad cast for me and then handed me the rod. I never took my eyes off my red-and-white bobber. It was there to teach me to recognize when a fish was tugging since I couldn't yet tell when the line was tight without it. When the bobber was tugged under, that was my sign a fish was on. So I stared. I watched it through the railing since I couldn't see over the top. I didn't take my eyes off my bobber for nothing.

Sometimes we would talk and sometimes not. Part of the joy of fishing is just sitting there, looking at water. For one calm, breezy hour after the next, I sat patiently. I don't know if it's normal for a six-year-old to just sit and sit like that, but I loved it. The water was dark brown, and I would stare at it for hours, quietly. I noticed the birds overhead, and I wondered, *How come the bird can see the fish and I can't?* I looked down into the brown water, and imagined the fish swimming around my bait, having a fish meeting, staring at the night crawlers and wondering, *Should I eat it? Should I not?*

Aunt Ernestine, a worrier, had called out, "Put a jacket on that baby," when we left the house earlier, even though it wasn't cold out, just a little cool, maybe. I considered slipping my arms out of the bulky coat, but I stayed put. I didn't take my eyes off my bobber. I knew one of those fish was going to say, "Lunchtime," and grab on.

Someone on the other side of the pier got a fish, and my dad shuffled over.

"Whatcha got there?"

They talked for a while. Then I heard him say, "Lemme get back to Jasmin." But my dad was a talker—still is—and I saw him lean on the railing, settle in a bit. "Well, now, lemme put it to you like this . . ." he said, and I knew he was going to be there for a while. But that was fine with me. I was in my happy place; the calm of safety and comfort washed over me. I watched my little red-and-white bobber, listening to the low, slow talk of my dad somewhere in the background, smelling the salt in the air. Dad and his friends seemed to know everything there was to know about fish:

which fish you could catch where, and when the fish would bite and when they wouldn't. When they talked about what they caught, they often used names different from the recognized common names. The dialect spoken by Black folks in the low country of South Carolina is heavily influenced by the Gullah Geechee creole language spoken by the descendants of enslaved Africans, so it's not uncommon for different names and terms to be used in our community.

Suddenly, my bobber dipped below the surface.

"I got one!" I shouted. My dad hurried over.

"Reel it in, Jazz!" he said. Just like he'd taught me, I pulled up sharply on the rod to set the hook in the fish's mouth and make sure it didn't slip off; then I reeled the line in as if my life depended on it. After a few moments, I saw a modest-size spot break the surface. I dehooked the fish and dropped it into the cooler. Beaming with pride, my dad reached over and gave me a high five.

"Way to go, baby girl!"

That evening, my grandmother Evelina fried up the fish we'd caught. She knew just what to do with every kind of fish we brought back and how to salt it so it didn't require refrigeration: first she sliced the fish at the backbone, then put salt directly on the fish and let it sit for two weeks so it wouldn't spoil; afterward, she'd rinse off the salt and then store it in water, with just enough salt so the fish floated. When we were ready to eat the fish, we'd soak it in fresh water overnight.

My grandmother was also a woman who loved to talk trash.

"That lil ol' thing, you coulda throwed that back," she

Baby Jasmin proudly holding up her
catch. Note the finger at the top of
the photo, classic parent move.

said, laying the cooked fish on a paper towel that covered a plate.

My dad laughed. "Wasn't much bitin' today."

"Can't even make a sandwich outta him," she said, pointing to the next one in the cooler, still over ice.

Finally, she turned around. Looked right at him. "Sidney," she said, "y'all ain't forget to put bait on them hooks, did ya?"

We all just cracked up.

My dad actually did catch a nice spot that day, but it wasn't quite legal size and so he let it go, per the regulations. My dad is low-key and smooth, moves with confidence and swagger.

He reels in fish with almost no struggle, just a lot of finesse. He held the fish in his hands. "Would you look at this," he said to me. We admired the fish for a bit and took a quick picture before releasing it.

Growing up in a fishing family taught me to appreciate the ocean for the life and sustenance it brings us. As a child, I had all these questions about what the fish were doing. "Why are fish here?" "How did you know they were here?" "Why are they hanging out by this pier?" "Why don't they go some-place else?" My dad and his family would answer my questions as best they could, and if they didn't know the answers, they always encouraged me to look for and find them. That's really where my curiosity about the ocean comes from.

Watching my dad and his friends gave me a different perspective from some other scientists working in marine conservation, who tend to see fishers like my dad as part of the problem. They think fishing can contribute to overhar-vesting, which is doing so much to deplete fish populations, throwing our ecosystems out of balance. While it's always hard to balance the needs of the marine population with human needs, and as much as I want to protect the life in our oceans, I never want that to be at the expense of subsis-tence fishers or their need to feed their communities. There's sufficient abundance for marine life to thrive while humans thrive, too.

In fact, it's more than enough if we are brave enough to look closely, understand what is happening, and ask ourselves honestly how to move forward. In my experience, that usu-ally takes a lot of time, effort, and mutual respect. I feel my work is all about proving that there is enough here for all of us; we simply have to find a sustainable way to use it. I know that it is possible for communities and conservationists to find a balance that works for the oceans: for the people who rely on them and the creatures that live there.

2

Field Season, Day Two

MISS Workshops Begin on the Research Vessel Garvin

Biscayne Bay, Florida

We push off at 5:30 a.m. Large predatory fish are often cre-
puscular, meaning they are most active at dawn and dusk.
The *Garvin* glides past a few party boats that are still at it
from the night before. The wind carries the thumps and beats
from club remixes over the water. Blinking blue and red strobe
lights pulse in one boat. Miami folks sure do love to party.

Once we get past the party section, all is quiet. I feel that
calm that comes only from being on the water. The world is
pitch-black except for the glow from the city in the distance.
The air smells crisp and is wet with dew. The steady hum of
the *Garvin*'s engine fills the otherwise silent air. Nick, one
of the Field School captains, turns the *Garvin*'s work lights
on: a beam as bright as the sun cuts across the deck and onto
the dark waters. I blink a few times until my eyes adjust and
then I smile: we could be outlaws on the high seas, or Navy
SEALs about to do a secret mission—everyone with their
hoodies on and looking so serious, ready for a full day of
fishing for sharks. In a way that I never have been before, I'm
surrounded by people who look like me.

The view of sunrise over Miami from
the research vessel *Garvin*

All of the research vessels I work on typically set fifty to
seventy hooks on a longline, but, unlike most research boats,
the *Garvin* is primarily a teaching vessel, and thus we set only
twenty-two hooks so as not to overwhelm the students with
large numbers of sharks. This is important when you are
working with trainees, who are just getting the hang of the
gear and shark-workup procedures.

I begin the introduction and instructions for the day.

"Today, we'll be fishing for sharks with a longline. Along the
line we'll attach twenty-two gangions (about two meters of

monofilament with a hook at the end) with a special clip called a tuna clip. With longlines we generally catch smaller fish."

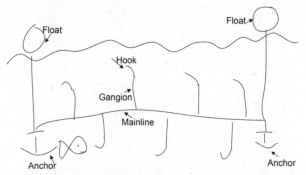

Clearly I'm *not* an artist. This is a drawing I made to help a friend visualize what longline gear looks like when deployed.

In my mind, I think, *Bonnetheads, bonnetheads. I hope we catch some bonnetheads.* The more I catch on the *Garvin,* the better chances we have of collecting enough samples for a proper dataset of at least fifty or sixty from this location. As an independent scientist without a PhD, I'm not able to apply for the grants earmarked for projects led by people with a doctorate, which means that I really need to make the most of my time on boats already funded for one purpose or another. I recently won the World Wildlife Conservation Leadership Award, and I'm putting that funding toward some extra surveys in Tampa next month. But here, I am really relying on the *Garvin* days to make it happen.

The students watch attentively and take notes. They are so focused that when they help to deploy the longlines in the water, all goes extremely smoothly. I shake out my arms, which are burning from the exertion, and I let out a deep sigh. I love the muscle burn.

"Up high," I say as I grab a high five from each student. "I am so impressed. You nailed it. On your first time. And in the dark, too!"

The whole group of them are smiling with pride. I take a seat next to a few participants to chat, while we leave the lines to soak for an hour. Instead of status-posturing or making people feel powerless or dumb, as so often happens in scientific research settings, we make sure to support and respect everyone.

When it's time to haul in the first line, I grab the floats with the boat hook and begin hauling in. About five hooks clear the water, empty. Then I see a nose.

"Shark on!" I say.

Carlee has the stopwatch around her neck and begins timing. Amani picks up the data sheet and records the time: *Shark on 7:01 a.m.*

I can tell from the shadow that it is a small animal and as it's drawn closer to the surface, I can see the telltale shovel shape of its head. I barely suppress a delighted squeal. It's an adorable bonnethead! This little guy measures in at barely over sixty centimeters. I swear, these guys are so small down here. They're little string beans in Biscayne Bay, as opposed to the ones that are dark and meaty and hefty in Tampa.

"Land on three," Catherine says, signaling the count to pull the shark aboard.

Catherine grew up in New Jersey, but, like me, she used to spend summers in coastal South Carolina with her relatives. At age seven or eight, Catherine had an encounter with a shark that made a big impression on her. She was in South Carolina at the beach with her family when an amateur fisherman caught a bonnethead by accident. A ripple of panic went around the beach—*There are sharks in the water! Get the children out of the ocean!*—but little Catherine went over to take a look at the bonnethead lying there on the sand, and saw that it was tiny. It was at that moment that Catherine realized that sharks weren't dangerous, that she didn't need to be scared of them, and that if someone was in trouble, it was the shark on the hook.

After that, she borrowed a book from her elementary school library about sharks and carried it around until the pages began to fall out. She told her dad that she wanted to either be a marine biologist or clean the shark tank at Sea-World. The problem was that the best classes she took in high school weren't science classes, so she ended up at a liberal arts college as a history major. It wasn't until she won a fellowship to conduct independent research abroad that Catherine decided that if she was going to study anything in the world, it was going to be sharks. She traveled to Australia, the Bahamas, Mozambique, and South Africa, looking at the many ways sharks and humans interacted, before ending up at the University of Miami, where she is now an assistant professor in marine conservation biology and ecology.

"One . . . two . . . three," she calls out now from the deck of the *Garvin*. Amani and I grab the shark and carry it carefully over to the cooler that we use to work up smaller sharks. "Gills dry," I call out; Carlee clocks it on the stopwatch; Jaida marks it on the data sheet: *Gills dry 2 mins and 5 seconds*. We stick a PVC pipe in the shark's mouth and turn on the pump, so ambient seawater starts flowing over its gills.

"Blood one," Catherine calls out. And, in our quick, smooth way, we go through the workup, taking blood samples to measure the shark's stress levels, muscle tissue to send out to the lab to determine what the hammerheads eat, and fin clips to determine the genetic makeup of this particular fish.

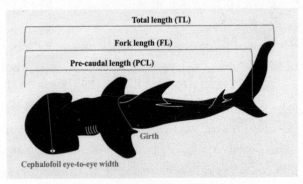

Kathy Liu created this image for her thesis to
illustrate each of the measurements we take
on the bonnetheads for this project.

We also take five specific measurements to describe these fish with extreme accuracy. The standard measurements are the pre-caudal length, or snout to the shark's "ankle"; fork length, or snout to the fork in the tail; total length, or snout to tip of tail; and girth, or "armpit to armpit." In addition to the standard measurements, we'll also take several measurements of the cephalofoil, which is the wide, bizarre part of the hammerhead's head. So Kathy takes a quick picture of each side of the cephalofoil against a gridded board before we release it, and everyone high-fives and congratulates one another on a solid workup.

Kathy Liu taking a photo of a bonnethead
on the "bonnethead board" while Amani
Webber-Schultz holds the animal

I do a happy twerk across the deck of the boat and sing, "We just got a bonnet, we just got a bonnet," in a conga rhythm.

Later in the day, we catch and work up a bunch of small nurse sharks. Nurse sharks are largely nocturnal and bottom-dwelling, and they max out at about two and three-quarters meters. They're pretty grumpy animals, in my opinion, but they're cool because they can breathe even while they're not moving. It's actually a common misconception that *all* sharks need to be moving at all times to breathe. There is such a wide variety of adaptations among all the species of sharks— yet another reason sharks are rad! Nurse sharks do what is called buccal pumping, using their cheek muscles to create a suction in their mouths, like a vacuum, moving water over their gills while sitting still. Other types of sharks are what we call obligate ram ventilators, meaning that they have to keep swimming to breathe. One of the benefits of longlines is that they allow the sharks to continue swimming around once they are on the line, which is obviously very important for those sharks that need to swim to breathe.

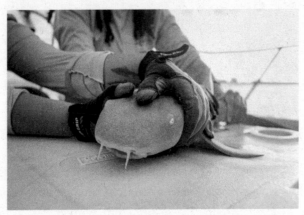

A baby nurse shark! Very cute, but full of rage.

One thing I am most proud of about MISS is that all of our programs, including this workshop, are all-expenses-paid. Finances are never a barrier for a student to attend or have this early career experience. And I am doubly proud that we can offer this introduction in such a top-of-the-line facility. It's gorgeous, and there is no reason all of these students shouldn't have access to the best. One of the biggest parts of my job for MISS is raising money, and that is because everything we offer is always free for participants. Not having money shouldn't be a reason you never get to have this experience on the water, with these buccal-pumping masterpieces.

· · ·

The first time I held a shark, I was eighteen. It was the summer after my freshman year, and I was out on a small boat with a team of three, motoring through the backwaters of tidal creeks in Charleston, South Carolina, surveying the area to catch and tag sharks. I was a science major and had done science in a lab before, but this internship was my first scientific fieldwork of any kind.

As we set out that early morning, the sun had yet to rise, so I couldn't see much as we pulled away from land, but the bow of our simple vessel tilted up toward the brightening horizon, charging forward with all the anticipation I felt in the moment. The thick, sulfurous smell of the local pluff mud was in the air and excitement was building in my chest.

Out on the boat, Bryan, the team leader, explained how we were going to catch the sharks using gill nets, which are mesh nets weighted at the bottom with a line of floats at the top, and drumlines, which are a single line weighted down with a large drum that acts as an anchor.

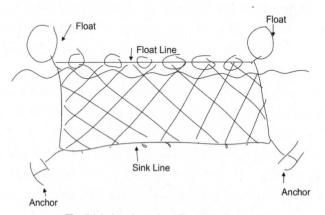

(Terrible) drawing of a gill net to show what
the gear looks like when deployed

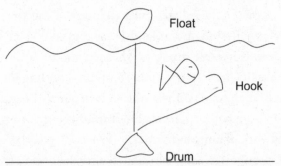

This shows what drumline gear looks like when it's deployed.
This is the last of my drawings I will subject you to, I promise.

We lowered the drumline into the water, then went to set the gill net and waited. At first, looking out over the water, I found it hard to imagine life below the surface; all was still and dark. Once we cut the low purr of the small motor on our boat, even the air was filled with silence. As we sat, I became increasingly aware of occasional ripples of movement. The first shark we pulled up was a bonnethead, with its distinctive head. I watched as the team worked the shark up the line toward us and was immediately enamored of its beauty. Its body was gray with a white underbelly, about one meter long, with two dorsal fins on top, two pectoral fins in the front, and two pelvic fins in the back. Bryan put the shark carefully on a measuring board to record its exact size, snipped off a small piece of the trailing end at the base of its dorsal fin for genetic testing, inserted a tag under the first dorsal fin, and determined she was female. I was impressed by how he controlled the hammerhead, an easier feat than it would have been with a much bigger fish. Bonnetheads are one of the smallest members of the hammerhead shark family—a great hammerhead, for example, can grow to an average of four meters, and other hammerheads, like scalloped hammerheads and smooth hammerheads, can be a variety of sizes in between.

Once the team attached the tag on the bonnethead and finished taking samples, it was time to return her to the water. In comparison to other sharks, hammerheads can get stressed very easily, and it's imperative to get them back into the water as quickly as possible so they can still recover. When Bryan turned to me and asked, "Would you like to release her?" I couldn't believe it. I had been prepared to simply observe, and here I was being entrusted with the vital task of releasing the bonnethead. Bryan carefully showed me how to hold and release the shark. Then he picked her up from the board and handed her to me. For the brief moment I held her, I was surprised at how rough her skin felt. I'd expected it to feel smooth, like a dolphin's skin, but sharks have hard scales known as dermal denticles, which are made of the same calcified material as teeth and feel rough under your palms. She was so strong, and I was awed by the power of the muscles I could feel tensing throughout her body. As I carefully released the shark back into the water with her new tag for identification, she gave a slight wiggle of her tail toward me, then took off quickly out of sight.

That animal was like none other I had known before. And, weirdly, I felt an instant affection or even love for her. I hadn't ever really thought much about sharks before, although I knew the popular, negative perception of them. But this silly thing we'd caught and released was nothing like that. She was little, and, frankly, seemed so vulnerable in our hands, all muscle and hydrodynamic perfection, yet she was also a stress case—with lactate in her heart that might fill up faster than she could process it if we didn't let her go fast enough. I've always been someone who roots for the misunderstood and for the underdog, and watching the shark swim away that day, my heart went out to her.

At the same time, the negative stereotypes and fearmongering surrounding these creatures felt eerily familiar to me as someone who's grown up Black in a country where we're assumed to be threatening, even when we're just minding our own business. I am generally very low-key and honestly have no grand plan to set the world right, but when people hurt me, I push back. I don't just take it. For many, it seems, this makes me an angry Black woman. But in a culture so steeped in white supremacy that to say, "Black lives matter"—not that they are superior, just that they matter enough to not be killed without legal recourse—is considered anti-American, it's a daily navigational challenge to maintain my personal boundaries so that I don't just collapse under the weight of so much routine microaggression, exclusion, and unkindness. When Black women fight back, we are seen as the enemy, just like sharks, which, more often than not, bite only when provoked. They are just trying to live.

This experience in the tidal creek, holding a shark for the first time, was the beginning of my journey to discovering my passion for sharks, which changed my life forever. And, most amazingly, it all happened somewhat by chance. It's crazy to think how much of my journey in shark science is the result of happenstance.

3

Day Three on the *Garvin*
MISS Workshops Continue

On the *Garvin,* we lead with love and encouragement, with respect and teamwork. We aim to show the students that while they are doing science, they should and can expect respect and encouragement rather than disrespect and abuse. The atmosphere we create in our MISS workshops is not the norm, sadly. On the second night of the workshop, we let the workshop participants ask us anything they want to help them navigate the trickier sides of shark science. We call this session Real Talk:

"Who was the professor anonymously accused in that article?"

We tell them.

"How much do you make?"

We tell them.

"Does anyone know about Dr. Minion's lab?"

This, of course, is not his real name. But it's what I will call him since he is awful and ridiculous.

I knew this question was coming. Before the workshop, I reviewed the participants' applications. I was moved by the passion of one woman, who is a member of the Suqua-mish Native American tribe of Kitsap County, Washington, which has lived on a peninsula off Washington State long before there was a Washington State. I felt an instant connection to another student who wrote how she loved scalloped hammerheads because of her Ecuadorian father's childhood stories about the Galápagos, where there's a huge scalloped-hammerhead migration. But my heart dropped when I noted that there was one applicant who hoped to work with a certain Dr. Minion. Just the thought of him makes my face and ears burn and my teeth tingle.

"Oh, boy," Jaida says. "I'll let Jasmin answer this one."

I struggle momentarily. I hate speaking ill of people. But this man is horrible, and choosing an adviser is important. He had thankfully *not* been my adviser, as I had been warned about him as an undergraduate student and tried to avoid him, though I was not altogether successful at that.

"I had a truly awful experience with him," I say and laugh, to keep from crying. "We had a dispute about my data, and I felt bullied into handing it over after he had people come after us for not being collaborative by sharing years of my work."

"Oh my god," the student says.

"Steer clear of him if you can. He's totally unethical, in my opinion."

I'd been working on a project tracking the movements of large juvenile and adult smalltooth sawfish at the time. I'd even won a prestigious grant to fund it, and I was uncovering new information about where these critically endangered animals spent their time. That's when Minion decided to help himself to my data and use it to publish an article that was inaccurate—pure bad science. I had been collecting data for years, and he scooped it up and published his (misleading) conclusions first.

When I first met Catherine, I told her all about my experience with Dr. Minion, and how unbelievable it was that his bad behavior had gone unchecked. That's when she told me about her own experiences being a woman in shark science. Back in 2020, shortly after I met her, Catherine funneled some of these experiences into an article she published in *Scientific American* called "The Dark Side of Being a Female Shark Researcher." In it, she shows that although more than 60 percent of graduate students in our field are women, shark science is still a "boys' club," with the majority of senior scientists being white men, and where there is rampant misbehavior of men toward women. She describes how, early in her career, she was "sexually assaulted, openly masturbated at, and verbally harassed" in professional settings. She notes that a 2013 survey across scientific disciplines found that 64 percent of respondents reported they had been sexually harassed during fieldwork, and 20 percent had experienced sexual assault. She remembers a male shark scientist—whom she'd considered her hero—telling a TV crew that he got into the field only because of the "beautiful green-eyed assistants," while pointing at her. She describes her first research talk at the annual American Elasmobranch Society (AES) conference, where a senior male scientist lobbed questions at her so aggressively during the Q and A that another male scientist actually apologized—later, of course, in private—saying, "He does that to a female graduate student every year or two."

(At least one woman he decided to grill left the podium in a flood of tears.) At this same conference, the closing banquet included a fundraiser where, as Catherine describes it, "scantily clad female graduate students were expected to parade auction items around the room," and a "dinner at which one senior scientist demanded to sit with only the 'prettiest' students, and an alcohol-fueled mixer where women needed to be on constant guard against roaming hands."

It was this enraging behavior and lack of accountability in academia that led to Catherine starting the Field School. The founding document was a sticky note that read NO A**HOLES.

I tell the Real Talk group to check out Catherine's article if they haven't already. It is a good overview of the crappier side of the field they are trying to break into, and they should know.

Like Catherine, I'm a member of AES, and this group represents what is right and wrong with so much of our field. When I joined the organization back in graduate school in 2017, I was the only Black attendee at their conference that year. I'll never forget sitting in the annual business meeting, where members discuss any changes to the organization. I was already pretty uncomfortable, since this was my first time at the conference, I didn't know anyone, it was still very early in my career, and no one else looked like me. And then I found myself in a room full of white people—the majority of whom were older men—discussing whether the organization needed a code of conduct around touching others without consent or bullying, harassing, or discriminating against other members. *What? Shouldn't that be a given?* But, in fact, it was so much not a given with the group that it became a matter of intense debate. Before I knew it, I was watching grown adults yell at one another about whether they should have a basic *code of conduct.* There was one other person of color in the room. We did not know each other, but we exchanged a silent glance that screamed out, *What on earth have we gotten ourselves into?* At one point during the conference, someone called her an "affirmative action attendee," among other little gems, and I get why she chose not to return the following year. I've remained a member ever since, and I've gone back to the conference each year, largely because my master's adviser was the president at the time; and because there are also a lot of folks who are pushing back and working hard for change within the society.

Shortly after Catherine's article came out and MISS entered the scene, an AES member keen to see change nominated me for election to the board of the society. I accepted the nomination, but, mysteriously, my name never made it onto the ballot. The whole situation was a bit sketchy, if you ask me. The way AES is set up, it's the nomination committee that ultimately decides who is on the ballot, a process that is not at all transparent and leaves a lot of room for bias. I feel that if someone is nominated, and if the nomination is accepted, then people should have a chance to vote for that person. At the very least, there should be clear guidelines as to how the decision is made about who gets on the ballot. But I suspect there were people who were scared of the idea of me on the board and what that might mean.

This year, someone has nominated me again; this time, I *am* on the ballot—and I want to win. With MISS, I'm committed to making change from the outside, and if I'm elected to the board of AES, I would be able to make change from the inside, too. I don't even know if I want to be on the "inside," if the inside is filled with too many sea snakes, but change happens when you come at the problem from multiple directions. If I'm elected to the board, it will mean the tides are turning. The vote will happen over the next three months and the results will be shared at our annual conference in July. I'll find out soon enough.

"I truly can't wait for the day when MISS no longer needs to exist," I say to the MISS group, "when we don't need to fight to be heard or create a safe space. But, until then, we are here to help insulate you as much as we can from the BS we had coming up. On our member resources page on the MISS website, we keep a running document that any member can contribute to about their *experiences*—the good ones and the hurtful ones. This document is meant to be nonjudgmental. A MISS member can't disparage a professor or program by saying 'They suck' but they can say 'This was my experience,' and give evidence of what happened. You'll note that some professors, departments, and institutions are on both lists. One member may have had an experience that made them uncomfortable with a lab, and yet another had a positive experience there. Being an ally isn't a set thing; it is rooted in individual acts and behaviors. People are complex. What one person is willing to put up with, another may not. So do research to learn as much as you can about any place before you go, and know that you have us to back you up."

The room erupts with hoots and hollers when I finish this impromptu speech. We stay up chatting into the night, and the talk moves away from questions into group venting, sharing, and healing. We sit around the table in the salon and laugh and yell and drop f-bombs as the water gently laps against the side of the boat.

Just as I did when I was a kid, I think about the fish under the water, like that bonnethead we caught and released today. I love how he almost certainly doesn't feel shame or guilt or sadness that he has that weird head and that we caught him to check it out. The moment we let him go, he just S-curved away from the boat, slow and steady, to continue his journey north, most likely. He may not know *why* he does what he does but he does it with such forward-facing purpose; he knows that it is right and necessary and he keeps moving, just as his ancestors have done for hundreds of millions of years.

Bennett, I decide to call him.

Not our pal Bennett but another friend, a nurse
shark, demonstrating sharks' trademark S-curve

We will almost certainly never meet again. Bennett may be re-caught, and the tag we put on him will encourage those who catch him to contact us to report the recapture. But regardless, that little bonnethead swims around the back of my mind before bed, when I'm idle and my thoughts swirl tirelessly. I ponder how far north he will travel and how changing water temperatures might affect his movements. Perhaps he will venture farther, perhaps he will stay closer to home. So many questions. But that's where science begins: with questions.

. . .

Throughout my childhood summers in Myrtle Beach, my father and I would go out to the pier and fish, and I'd ask him all sorts of questions and he'd tell me all sorts of stories. Stories about the resiliency of our family, and how we Grahams have always made a way for ourselves in the world.

After a long day fishing, we would visit Broadway at the Beach, a big tourist area by the waterfront, with a shopping complex, museums, activities, and restaurants. There was an aquarium, Ripley's, where I would sometimes go and stand under the glass tunnel in the shark tank to look up at the bellies of fish swimming overhead and all around me, never realizing I would one day devote my life to studying them. To get there, we had to walk by a mini-golf course called Dragon's Lair, with a giant, fire-breathing dragon inside a volcano overlooking the walking path. Most of the time the dragon was hidden inside the volcano, but every thirty minutes, a puff of fire sputtered out of the cone, and the dragon would stick its head out, swiveling in jerky, robotic motions, threatening passersby and blowing smoke and fire out of its mouth.

I was always an anxious child, and I was flat-out terrified of that dragon. But the dragon was unavoidable if you wanted to get to the boardwalk, where you could feed the giant carp, which I also loved, so I would make my dad speed-walk past the mini-golf course, and time our route so we weren't near the dragon when it emerged.

But feeding the giant carp was not nearly as exciting as catching our own fish off the pier. Not only did I enjoy fishing, but I also enjoyed spending quality time with my dad. We'd talk and he'd tell me the stories about our family, to teach me a bit, I think, about how to face the world, to be brave, and to realize that you have to see the dragons for what they are.

As a child growing up in Harlem in the 1960s, without running water, moving into government subsidized housing in the Hill was a big step up in my dad's eyes because they had not only running water but heat! Not to mention a real bathroom instead of an outhouse. And he certainly wasn't poor in any of the ways that mattered: he was rich in love and community. His family was among the most "well-off," relatively speaking, in the neighborhood, because they had indoor plumbing. Everyone else had to use an outhouse in the back. It wasn't until he joined the army that my father realized how much less he and his community had than everyone else, and that for most people, indoor plumbing was a standard thing.

Since the Hill was cut off and isolated by the white, segregated Myrtle Beach, my family and our neighbors took care of one another because it was the only way to survive. My grandparents and their neighbors fished not just for pleasure but also for sustenance, for food. Before social scientists coined the term *food desert*, the Hill was exactly that, and so we went to the water. My grandmother was the real fisher of the family, always making sure she came home with the biggest fish and the most fish, making certain she "won," as she liked to say. A person who had a good fishing day might have someone else cook it and then everyone would share it. And while one woman was fishing, another woman in the neighborhood would watch the children, and in this mutual way, people got by.

My paternal grandfather, Ernest Graham, was one of the only Black business owners—maybe the only one—in the white part of segregated Myrtle Beach, and it was a whole thing. When he was young, he worked for Mr. Benfield, who owned a gas station, Benfield Esso, that later became Benfield Exxon. When Mr. Benfield passed away, he willed the gas station to my grandfather and great-uncle because he felt like they worked really hard and cared about it, while his children didn't seem to care much. The gas station was in the white part of town, and knowing that people suck, and racism is a thing, Mr. Benfield also preemptively paid for a lawyer to fight when people inevitably tried to take the station from them.

My family had so many run-ins with the Klan. But they've never taken anything passively, and they have always been super involved in the community in Myrtle Beach. My great-grandfather Luther Graham Sr. was involved in the Myrtle Beach chapter of the NAACP, plus he was a member of the Oddfellows as well as the Eastern Stars, and he and my

The original sign that was outside
my grandfather's gas station

grandfather were charter members of the Prince Hall Masons in Myrtle Beach in 1941.

Luther Graham Sr. also started Bellamy and Graham's funeral home, which provided funeral services to our community. But seeing as the (white-run) ambulances wouldn't go into Black areas, my family also became known as a sort of rescue squad, transporting people in their hearse for reasons other than just death. Instead of leaving their fellow community members to suffer and die when the white ambulances wouldn't show up, they began taking the sick or injured to the hospital. Luther's work had a real spiritual mission to it— do unto others—and in fact on my dad's side of the family there are several pastors, including Antny Graham, who founded the True Vine Missionary Baptist Church in an area of Conway (north of Myrtle, and which used to be called Grahamville). Many of the Grahams have been pastors of that church and several other churches in Horry County.

My grandmother was a housekeeper for the Chapin family for a while, and that, too, provided some stability and protection for our family. Like many small towns in America, Myrtle Beach had the city officials who *technically* ran the town, and then there were the wealthy families, the Southern aristocracy—in this case, the Burroughs and the Chapins—who *actually* ran Myrtle Beach.

Eventually, though, my grandfather's gas station went out of business. It wasn't due to intimidation, but gentrification. He owned the franchise, but he leased the building that housed it, and eventually he couldn't afford the lease anymore. If you drive by the lot today, there's a Maryland Fried Chicken franchise where the gas station once stood.

After the gas station closed, my grandfather went to work as a mechanic at Sears. It was maybe around this time that one of my grandfather's brothers, Sammy, died after a car wreck. The hospital wouldn't mix races for blood donations, and they couldn't find a Black blood donor to match his rare blood type. So he died from a lack of blood, which should have been entirely avoidable. This idea may seem like a horrible thing of the past, but it's really not so different from recent laws in some states that compel doctors to let women die carrying out a fatal pregnancy, rather than terminate the pregnancy, so it's clear America is still enforcing legally cruel and unusual oppression for some. Dad would tell me these things in a very matter-of-fact way. But when I imagine the doctors who took an oath to do no harm just standing there and watching my great-uncle expire, it physically hurts. Something builds like sediment over my heart. I don't know where that hurt and anger went for my grandfather or father, but even generations down the line, it doesn't just go away.

These were the stories I grew up on. One of my dad's favorites to tell was about the night my grandpa Ernest was standing in front of a club in Harlem called the Rainbow Inn when the KKK drove through, crosses burning. Ernest stayed put, unwilling to concede to the Klan that they could scare him out of his own neighborhood.

The Klansmen were on their way to Charlie's Place, a nightclub that was a popular stop on the chitlin circuit, where some of the best acts performed for Black people during the Jim Crow era. It had many of the greats come through: Ella Fitzgerald, Billie Holiday, Ray Charles, Little Richard, the Temptations, and Marvin Gaye. The celebs would play the big hotels in Myrtle Beach, going in and out through the back, and then they'd head over to Charlie's and perform for everyone excluded from the hotels. The shag, which is the state dance of South Carolina, actually originated in Charlie's Place.

White teenagers started coming to the club because they had heard about all the acts that came to Charlie's, and the owner, Charlie Fitzgerald, wouldn't—or at least didn't—turn them away. So it was integrated most nights, and soon word got out.

When the Klan arrived at Charlie's Place, they beat Charlie and clipped his ears. The Black people inside fought back. They shot at the invaders; one Klansman was killed. When they removed his robe and hood, they could see his Conway City police uniform underneath. Some people thought they had recognized the chief of police riding in the front of the first car. So it's unsurprising that no one was brought to justice. The Klan wasn't punished for the attack and no one from the neighborhood was punished for killing the Klansman. The city just threw its hands up and said, "Well, that happened."

Whenever my dad would tell the story about that night, I would always love the ending. "When the Klan drove back through Harlem, fleeing from the shots, your grandfather was still at the club, and he said the Klan were flying by. . . . They were driving so fast to get outta there, their crosses blew out."

My dad is one of the most intelligent people I know, though he always downplays it because school was never really his thing and he didn't go to college. I soaked up my dad's wisdom like a sponge and I carry it with me to this day. You may not get what you want, but you can and should fight for what you need. How you fight depends on who you are—but the important point is, you never just take it. Every day, I try to practice what he taught me, with the help of my community and mutual respect: to be brave in the face of dragons.

4

On the Research Vessel *Garvin*
MISS Workshops Continue

"Do you like my shoes?" Jaida says as she greets the next round of MISS students the following weekend in the *Garvin*'s salon. It's 7:30 a.m. and we're checking folks in for the workshop.

The student does a double-take and bursts out laughing. The shoes are slides in the shape of bright-blue fish with yellow bellies, and her toes stick out of the mouths, like wiggly tongues. They're truly awful shoes. Jaida always wears them at these workshops.

"I low-key love how ridiculous they are," the participant says, grinning.

"Do not encourage her," I say as I pass by to stand next to Carlee, who is sitting by the TV. She sips her coffee from an insulated mug and holds it with both hands while staring into it silently. She is not a morning person. Of the four MISS co-founders, she and I may be most alike in temperament: we are both introverts, but never wallflowers. When Carlee starts her day, she does it dressed to impress—shiny pink box braids flowing, long acrylic nails popping.

Keeping it light with Amani Webber-Schultz
and Jaida Elcock on board the *Garvin*

The mood on the *Garvin* is electric and exciting. The participants are standing up, leaning against the counter, or sitting around the large table, where an unfinished card game from last night sits, their notebooks out, eager and ready. I scan the room, and even after all this time, I feel a funny pain at how rare it is to be in a science space like this: it's full of people of color and I'm not alone. Catherine sees Carlee with her mug and makes a beeline for the coffeepot. She is baffled that three of the four MISS co-founders (all but Carlee) are tea drinkers. She fills her tiny cup, sporting a sawfish sticker, with probably her second or third cup of coffee.

I pull Kathy aside; I want to see how she's doing with our methodology so far. "How was using the bonnet board?" I ask.

"Yeah, easy. Totally natural," she says. "I'm not sure how ImageJ will go, but placing and photographing the hammers on the board is easy."

To compare the bonnetheads in Biscayne and Tampa and see if they are as different as they appear to the naked eye, we're paying close attention to the cephalofoil shape and size.

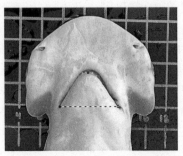

Photo of bonnethead cephalofoil against
the gridded bonnethead board

The form and structure of a shark is called its morphology. The typical way marine biologists might measure fish in the field involves using super-expensive equipment that takes a photograph of the fish and a measurement simultaneously, in a process called laser photogrammetry. Here the researcher programs the desired measurement (for example, the precaudal length) and the camera uses two beams of light at the set distance to take the measurement as it takes the photographic image as well. But because being an independent researcher also means being a broke researcher, I figured out a way to measure the cephalofoil that is just as good as the laser photogrammetry but costs me only three dollars. I use a regular cell-phone camera to take a picture of the cephalofoil and put the image into a free computer program called ImageJ that allows me to then take measurements of the head on the computer, pixel by pixel. I made a background board to place under the head, so that when we take a picture, the head will be on a grid, which is necessary when using ImageJ for the purposes of providing a scale.

"No worries; once we're back at dock, I'll teach you ImageJ. You'll be great."

I've already picked up that Kathy is super conscientious and always finds a way to figure out what she doesn't know, so I'm not worried about this step.

Our creative workaround (fingers crossed that it *will* work) is also better for the fish, because we keep them out of the water only as long as it takes us to snap one photograph, instead of prolonging that time taking a bunch of measurements.

"And are you all clear on how to label the muscle samples for Sora's lab?" I ask.

Kathy nods.

"Great," I say, "we'll store them in the Field School's freezer until we have a decent number and then send them to Sora in California."

Dr. Sora Kim is a MISS member who runs a lab at the University of California, Merced, and she offered to run a stable isotope analysis on our muscle tissue. We rely on the mutual support MISS members give one another; otherwise, we wouldn't be able to do what we do. Sora has extra money, and she offered to do the analysis in her lab and cover the cost of processing the samples, as well as of shipping the samples to her. These results will teach us what the bonnets are eating, so we can see if diet differs between these two locations and if that disparity is what's driving their differences in size.

Sora's a perfect example of the MISS way: be different, think different. Geologists use stable isotopes to date things like fossils, and Sora, who is a geologist by training, was among the first to figure out how to apply this tool to sharks. Since energy is transferred up the food chain, organisms that photosynthesize are known as primary producers. They'll have a certain ratio of carbon and nitrogen isotopes because of how they process the sun; then, animals that eat them will have a shifted ratio of stable isotopes, and so on. We can, therefore, with Sora's method, tell where something is on the food chain and what it's eating, based on the stable isotopes in the muscle biopsy. Scientists can get very siloed, with a biologist using only one set of tools and another type of scientist using another set, but never cross-pollinating ideas, since we go to separate conferences, read separate journals, and conduct our work without much community. So many wasted opportunities!

"And," Kathy says, "I have the fin clips labeled, too."

"Awesome," I say. I'm feeling good about heading to Tampa soon to start collecting there, since it seems Kathy is really capable and well set up here in Biscayne to continue her half of the work.

The rest of the group settles, and Amani explains the plan. "We'll be doing a shark survey today, which means we go out and fish for sharks in the area—see what's in these waters and measure them, see how they are doing. We may catch some blacktips, some nurse sharks, and maybe—hopefully for Jasmin—some bonnetheads."

"When we pull a shark on, MISS co-founders will restrain

I'm on the right, helping workshop participants bait hooks
in preparation to deploy a longline during a 2021 survey.

the shark by holding it down at the head, mid-body, and tail,
and once we are ready, you can step onto the platform and
get right up next to the animals to collect samples.

"Communication is key," Amani continues. "You don't
want someone to lift a shark's tail to draw blood, for example,
when the person at the head isn't ready. On some research
vessels people think that screaming and cursing is how you
communicate. But not here. We talk to one another—
'Ready?'—and we listen. This way, we are on the same page
and we are respectful."

Shortly before nine, we reach our first fishing spot, Bear
Cut (an area supposedly named because someone saw bears
swimming across the pass, but you know how these old sea
tales get spun sometimes). And on our first haul, we're in
luck.

It's a scalloped hammerhead! Scalloped hammerheads are
larger than bonnets and have much wider heads. They get the
scalloped part of their name because their heads are bumpy

(a.k.a. scalloped), not smooth, along the front edge of the hammer.

Our first participant walks onto the platform, and her body is literally shaking with excitement. It still makes me smile. I love being able to give this experience to people. Amani is over the dorsal fin, and she helps the participant find the piece of skin where she will tag the animal, just under the dorsal. As if she's using an ear-piercing gun, the participant attaches the long tag without hesitation. The tag has an ID number and is the trademark blue that the *Garvin* and the Field School use.

Jaida writes down the ID number. We tag the animals so that if they are recaptured by anyone, we'll know. Using recapture rates, researchers can make calculations to determine the potential population size; we can also look at how much the animal has grown between captures.

The next participant comes, focused, to take a fin clip. Amani's hands are full holding down the mid-body, but she talks the participant through what she's doing—finding the small trailing end at the base of the dorsal fin and cutting it off. This cartilage contains genetic information, much like we might get from our fingernails. I can feel the shark's muscles contract under my gloved hands. I use all of my arm strength to keep the tail pinned down while the participant takes a small fin clip and swiftly puts the sample in a vial filled with solvent to preserve it.

"Oh my god! This is so cool!" she says. She pats the shark delicately like a dog as she stands up to leave. "*Good girl!*" she says, and then quickly takes the fin clip to Kathy.

The data from the fin clips will be processed by Kristina

Black, another MISS member and a student who can fold this into her graduate work and thus use her lab resources. She's going to run the genetics analysis on all the fin clips so that we can tell if the sharks are related to one another: Is there a lot of genetic mixing between the locations? Are they genetically distinct? Based on what she finds, we can see if the size differences are genetic—that is, if these tiny Biscayne Bay sharks look like bonnetheads but in fact are a cryptic species, or if they have very little genetic mixing with the larger population and are in fact a subpopulation.

"Biopsy," Catherine calls out, signaling for the next participant to come and take the next sample. This is the tissue sample that we'll send to Sora's lab to find out what they eat.

Next, we do a parasite check because a colleague of ours is doing a study on parasites, and it's easy for us to collect data. No parasites.

"Did we get the sex?" Catherine calls out. The participant who took the biopsy is still on the platform, so she checks if the hammerhead has claspers, which are two extended protrusions between the pelvic fins. Male sharks swim to one side or the other of a female and stick their claspers into the female's cloaca, an external opening for the urinary, digestive, and reproductive tracts; through the claspers, he deposits sperm. Shark sex is quite violent. Since they don't have hands, the male bites onto the female's back or pectoral fin to secure her, while the long claspers penetrate and then hook inside her cloaca opening, like grappling hooks. The female is often left with nasty scratches and marks after copulation. As a result, females have evolved a thicker skin than males.

"I don't see any claspers," the participant says. There are

indeed none, so the shark is a female. Jaida notes *female* on the data sheet.

"Measurements."

The next participant comes down to take the body measurements, and her hands are shaking with anticipation. Your first shark workup can be extremely nerve-racking, but despite her nerves, she goes through the list of measurements for the body (which we're taking separately from the specific and focused measurements we're doing of the crazy head of hammers we catch) and then moves off the platform. Since this is a hammerhead, Kathy comes down to take a quick picture of the head against the larger grid board I made for great and scalloped hammerheads so we can run the picture through ImageJ.

Measuring the total length of a shark
during a MISS workshop

When we're all done, Catherine announces that we are going to shift the shark to the edge of the boat on three. On her signal we carefully slide the animal forward. She gives us

Practicing taking measurements on Vanna White,
a stuffy great white shark we all love very much

one final countdown to release: "One . . . two . . . three," and we push. I am sure to keep the tail in my hand until it passes everyone's face (because getting pimp-slapped by a shark does *not* feel good—ask me how I know), and the shark slides gracefully into the water. It's a beautiful release: the hammerhead is kicking before it hits the water and swims away without hesitation, as if to say, *I'm outta here.* Release conditions are rated and recorded in the notes as Excellent, Good, Fair, Poor, or Dead on Arrival (DOA).

"Excellent," I call out. Jaida notes: *Release 10:10 a.m., Release Condition Excellent.* Like a synchronized-swimming team, we work with one another so well. Kathy comes out to let us know the final lactate level was 9.5, which is further affirmation that the workup was fast and didn't stress the fish out too much. This level is not bad for a large hammerhead species—the mean for us on the *Garvin* is 10.2 ± 1.4—but if another animal had lactate that high, we'd be concerned.

My muscles are aching from sitting on my knees and holding the shark—every shark workup I feel a little bit older. I stare down into the water a second more before I hear a "woot, woot" from someone. The mood on the *Garvin* is jubilant. High fives all around.

"You rocked," I hear one participant say to another.

"That was unbelievable—my gosh."

"I can't believe we just did that."

Around noon, we're ready to haul in our second set of drumlines. We catch two sandbar sharks, back-to-back. Sadly, no more hammerheads, but I love to give the participants experience with working up any shark. The Field School can use the data for some of their other projects.

After the third shark for the day, we wrap up the drumlines. We're done! We detach the float line from the drum, untie all of the floats from the line, and store the drums neatly back on the starboard side of the boat. Everyone is exhausted, hot, and sweaty.

"Jasmin," I hear Jaida call out as we glide back into the marina. "Your curls are popping today."

I'm wearing my natural curls in a voluminous Afro encircled by a black headband.

"What products do you use?"

I tell her I use Design Essentials, and she nods knowingly. Finding the right product for hair like mine, which is naturally very dry, is never easy when it's constantly being exposed to salt water, wind, and other elements.

It seems small, this exchange, but it is in fact huge.

Black hair is one of those things that seems to be judged and policed by white people, while this regulation is somehow also invisible to them. It's disorienting and confusing, when, during any number of activities, my hair is commented on. Once, one white colleague asked me, "Yesterday your hair was short and today it is long. Explain that to me? It's fascinating."

"It's Black girl magic," I said.

He chuckled. "But, really, it's fascinating. How is that possible?"

"It's Black girl magic," I repeated. In the flow of work, I didn't have time (or energy or desire) to answer a question I felt was inappropriate. How is "I'm wearing a weave" in any way relevant to our conservation efforts or going to make this interaction more comfortable for me? I can't communicate with someone who thinks they are curious but is in no way interested in changing or widening their perspective.

Natural, "kinky" hair—the thick and tight curly-curls that naturally grow out of my head—is often called unprofessional or improper in the workplace or at schools; or those who may be unconscious of their bias call it "wild," "crazy," or maybe even "ugly." The default mode when I was younger was to relax my hair. I was never trying to look white or de-Blackify myself with straight hair; relaxed Black hair is its own thing. I relaxed my hair because that's what Black women in my family did to look our best and to make life easier, perhaps on multiple levels. In the morning, relaxed hair can be quicker to style or manage than natural hair. Weaves and wigs offer variety and time for your hair to repair or rest from the chemicals in the products that are used to treat hair.

Many Black children get their hair relaxed after a certain age, like with getting their ears pierced. As a child, I loved walking out of the salon with fresh hair, feeling beautiful and perfect. But once water touches relaxed hair, the frizz is real. Then you have to do your hair again, which is time-consuming and can be expensive or require a trip to the salon.

When I was a kid, my mother would be very frustrated with me because I was constantly jumping into water. Swimming for many Black girls is off-limits. Time and money, interlaced with personal pride in looking good despite white ideals of beauty that reject our hair, prevents many Black children from enjoying the pleasures of the water. But since she knew I absolutely couldn't be kept from the ocean, my mom started to braid my hair in styles that would keep for the whole summer, so I could be carefree in the water without her getting frustrated. Of course, as a kid, I didn't know that this was a decision point—to move away from the default mode of pretty and permed hair. I didn't know how others might look at me differently with a head full of cornrows; I didn't know that there had been laws, not overturned until as late as the 1970s in some states, to prohibit enslaved and then free people from wearing braids the way I was doing; or that when many Africans were brought to America, their heads were shaved to prevent them from braiding their hair in ways that identified them with their tribe or home community. For me, braids just meant I could jump into the water without thinking. Such a "small" thing.

My hair is natural now, not permed, because it's easier for me to manage on the water than constantly worrying about my roots puffing up when wet and not matching the rest of my relaxed hair. I wear it natural most days in the offseason, too, with maybe a weave or wig for variety, but when I'm in my field season, I usually wear crochet braids or another protective style, to shield against the elements. It's not healthy to keep hair in a protective style too long—braids tugging on my roots can cause hair to break, too—so I add in the occasional hair-rest week, to let it breathe.

Today, it's in a natural Afro since my hair is on a break, and, as Jaida pointed out, it's looking nice—just there, on my head, while I do science. Being big and free, curling in whatever way that it wants to curl and being fully embraced.

Jake Jerome, Carlee Jackson Bohannon, and Jaida Elcock (*left to right*) work up a shark on the platform of the research vessel *Garvin*.

Everyone is different in how they try to fit into a space that isn't designed for them, or in how they interact with people who have a prejudice or even an unconscious bias against them. I was raised to set boundaries. I'm not going to engage if I think that a question implies cynicism or an underlying prejudice, because it takes up a lot of energy. We've had to fight to hold on to our houses, our land, our stories—to hand them down from one generation to the next, along with the knowledge of how to preserve them when we are systematically excluded or shunned from mainstream white institutions. My ancestors were never included in the census or written records until after the Civil War. In my family, we have Great-Aunt Sarah's Bible, where she recorded her family history.

Like historians trying to trace unrecorded Black history, shark scientists can face similar challenges. Sharks have a skeleton made of cartilage, a soft material that deteriorates; in other words, sharks don't leave much in the way of fossils behind them. The way paleontologists can find and reconstruct a whole dinosaur from prehistoric earth—that's not going to happen with a shark. The fossil record for sharks is very, very scarce—occasionally, a piece of shark lands in an underwater volcano and may fossilize, but it is rare. Mostly all we have are teeth and dermal denticles, which are modified teeth-like scales making up the shark's skin. But that's it.

This meager fossil record is part of why it's so hard for taxonomists and evolutionary biologists to agree on shark family trees. Their history is mysterious in many ways, but this makes it all the more important that we understand it. Just like the history of my family and other Black families in

America, we must piece it together as best we can with what we have, so that we can take that knowledge and apply it going forward.

The last business our family owned, the funeral home, closed in the 1970s, and the Myrtle Beach tourism industry became the best way—the only way, at that time—to make ends meet. The unrelenting machine of American racism kept on churning, cutting off our economic self-reliance at every turn, so a bunch of my great-aunt Carol's family got jobs at the Sands Ocean Club, including my great-uncle Baba (I don't know why everyone called him that, but that *was* what everyone called him) who was employed there the longest as a bell captain.

My dad worked there for a bit, too, as a bellhop, but he was doing airport security when he first laid eyes on my mother. She was traveling back from a temporary duty assignment for training for the air force. People were always trying to set her up with guys, because she was still single. Even though my mom didn't want to be set up, she humored her friends. Her friend who was picking her up saw my dad and said, "Oh, he's cute," and decided to introduce him to my mom. They exchanged numbers. He called, but she had already gone on leave. When she returned she had several messages from him. She called him back, they met for dinner at a restaurant, and the rest is history.

They are so different. My dad is a country kid at heart: he likes to hunt, hog-trap, fish, and be outdoors, letting slow, long days unfold and just chill. My mom likes to be indoors, maybe reading, nice and comfortable; outside of her element, she's afraid of everything, and doesn't like being in nature or getting hot. In the air force, she failed her shooting test six times before they pity-passed her, so hunting was not in the cards for her. Where Dad is direct, Mom takes a "bless your heart" approach in telling people things about themselves. Where my dad is low-key, if my mom does not constantly have things to do, she feels a gap in her soul.

After Luther Graham Sr. passed away, his property was divided up among his children. Eventually, part of this property came into the possession of my father. Some stayed and some moved away, but everyone held on to their piece except for my great-uncle Cecil. My great-aunt Sarah also owned some property right across from what used to be a landfill and then became a Sheraton. Now of course it is hot property and developers approached her for years trying to buy it, but she never sold because they forever offered us pennies compared to what they'll make. So we hold on to these houses— like my grandparents' home, which is boarded up—just to spite them.

To this day, our family continues to fight for our place in the world, to not be erased. In the early 2000s, there was a fire on one of the parcels of family land that my father owned and it burned down a trailer that was on it. My dad decided he would rebuild on the property with a permanent structure, a duplex, to rent out for income, since we lived in Columbia, South Carolina, at this time. Also, he felt building a solid structure would make it less likely that the city would try to take it, since it was always trying to eliminate our Black corner of white Myrtle Beach. Several years before, for example, my father had to sell a few feet of the property to the city so they could expand the road; otherwise, they would have condemned the property and taken it under eminent domain.

I was in middle school during my father's fight with the city, and although we weren't fishing as much then, we still had a lot of father-daughter time. He'd started working as a private investigator, which meant he had flexible hours, and so he would pick me up from school, and we'd usually have to go on a stakeout. I'd sit in the quiet and dark with him while he waited for some cheating husband to emerge and then snap the guy's picture.

My dad has had many jobs. He can do most anything. He is super handy, very observant, and a quick study. He's been a landscaper, worked in hospitality, was in the army, served as a police officer, sold houses, sold cars, and was a private investigator before he retired—the list goes on. My dad did all the research he could on eminent domain and learned that the city could invoke it only if there was absolutely no other way to do the public works that needed to be done. He was able to show that there was another way; so, in the end, he had to sell a sliver of land to the government but kept most of it intact.

"Jasmin," he'd tell me, "one day, that house will be yours and you need to know how to protect it."

5

At Home
Tampa, Florida

It's early morning, the beginning of month two of my first independent field season. I'm making a cup of tea in my kitchen and realizing I could get used to this new life of mine. If I thought I might miss the prestige, routine, and rigor of the academic track, the opposite is turning out to be true. Instead, I'm learning to value the change of pace, the spaces in my day—and my brain—that have opened up now that I'm not wrestling with constant stress and distress. I open the sliding door to my backyard, and Iggy, my little, short-haired white dog, shuffles along with me to the small bistro table and chairs sitting on the patio. I adopted Iggy back in graduate school: I was in a new place, experiencing a whole heap of new changes, and needed a companion to get me through it all. He's helped me through a lot of tough times. Iggy's overanxious like me, but I like to think we understand and help each other out.

A nice breeze blows through the backyard and ruffles the leaves on the tall trees; the hammock swings. It's not yet eight o'clock—I almost always wake up at seven-thirty. As I sip my

Igloo Graham (a.k.a. Iggy),
looking dapper in a bandanna

tea, I take in the small science shed I am building out here. It's a prefab structure I bought from Home Depot that looks like a miniature barn or a kids' clubhouse: inside, it is twelve feet by ten feet—space for me to build a one-person lab and work area. I recently used some grant money for this shed because it was getting increasingly difficult to find room for all my tools and equipment in my small, twelve-hundred-square-foot home, and I needed to create some separation between my living space and my workspace. Today, my friend Rebekah and I will install the insulation so the shed-lab will be fully functional by the end of the summer. A few weeks ago I had an electrician come and install power, so once the insulation is done I'll be able to install my portable air conditioner and the shed will be temperature-controlled. Then, I can finally move my freezer full of shark samples out of my

laundry room and into the shed. All of the bonnethead samples we collected on the *Garvin* will stay in the Field School
freezer until we send them out to Sora, but the samples we
collect here in Tampa, I'll store in my freezer.

I check my email to see if there is anything more from
the exchange between the board of the American Elasmobranch Society and its Equity and Diversity (E&D) Committee, which I'm a member of. The past few weeks have
been a flurry of heated email activity as the board voted to
decide if the E&D Committee can go ahead and apply for a
grant to do our work around making the organization more
welcoming and inclusive.

The latest kerfuffle started when our committee proposed
a few initiatives to make the conference and gala more comfortable for everyone, and the board said, "No, we don't have
the money to do it." This was odd, considering that quite a
few things we proposed didn't actually cost any money, like
changing the policy of placing alcohol in the center of each
table, a practice that had fueled a lot of bad behavior in the
past. At which point, I began to smell something fishy, as
did other E&D Committee members. We said that if lack
of money was the purported problem, then we'd apply for
a grant. And the board then said, "Well, no, you can't apply
for a grant without our permission." This was also interesting
to me, considering the previous president of AES had gone
off and applied for funding for his own personal podcast
through AES without asking board permission, but I digress.

Why would any reasonable person prevent our broke
group from trying to get more money? The emails were flying. One board member wrote that he didn't think the work

was important enough to warrant funding, citing specifically the DEI training we wanted all leadership members to take, for which I would be one of the facilitators: "Other than being a nice summer paid position for some, the big concern is we already have a difficult time getting people to volunteer their time to the society. Asking them to take unpaid training will further decrease the pool of people wanting to serve the society as volunteers. And it seems this is a big part of the grant proposal."

Remember the past president who applied for money to pay himself to start a podcast—without permission from the board? Yep, same guy. He applied as a representative of AES to do a podcast and then told leadership after the fact, *I got money from Save Our Seas, and I'm going to do this podcast. These are the people I'm going to have on this podcast* (who, by the way, were all his friends, most of them white men). Then he had the gall to say to us, Well, y'all are just doing this grant so you can have a nice paid summer job.

So I responded: "Yes, the DEI trainers get paid. And their travel is paid." As for the idea that requiring DEI training would deter people from volunteering for leadership positions, I noted that the training would be done during the annual meeting, when everyone was already present. It wasn't going to require additional time from anyone. "For the leadership, we can do it during a meeting, like a board meeting. It will take two hours. And as someone who is from a minority community and has attended AES, believe me, this is a valuable use of the leadership's time. And if they feel that learning how not to make this society a racist, sexist, ableist, homophobic, transphobic hellhole is not worth two hours of their time, they shouldn't be in leadership. If they don't want to put in work that benefits the society, perhaps they shouldn't be in charge of anything."

The board eventually voted 7–5 in favor of us applying for the grant. Oh, but wait—we were told we needed two-thirds, not a simple majority, and so no, we could not apply for a grant to fund our DEI work. The current AES president, Miki (who was on our side in this matter), forwarded those of us working on the grant the email chain that reflected the board's final decision. We were shocked at some of the comments that were made in that discussion; one principal investigator on the grant who saw more of the discussion thread than I did flagged comments that seemed to be in direct violation of our code of conduct (the one folks fought tooth and nail to pass) and considered reporting them, but ultimately did not.

Then a longtime member, Dr. Lisa Whitenack, who calls herself the "by-laws monkey," sleuthed out that we actually needed only a *simple* majority, which we had, because the item was proposed by a member at large, not a member of the E&D Committee, and we could indeed move ahead with applying for a grant. This morning, as I stand on the patio with Iggy, I see an email from Miki, confirming that Lisa was right and a simple majority could carry the vote. On a separate chain, one of the women who had long endured the inappropriate behavior that Catherine had shouted out in her *Scientific American* article, wrote to the group, "They've been outwitted! HA!"

If I am elected to the board at the AES meeting this year, I would be part of a group replacing outgoing members who are of the old guard, meaning our faction would suddenly have a supermajority. We would really be able to vote for change. And yet, rereading the email thread, I wonder if I actually want to be on this board at all. Why would I put myself through this? I've done so much work to move away from these kinds of institutions, to carve out my own space. Is it possible for AES to actually improve? I wonder if I should pull my nomination. I'm always up for helping to create change, but not if many of the people in the organization leadership don't really want it. I suspect that they're keen to look good—they don't want to be seen as racist or misogynist—but they have no intention or desire to actually be inclusive of people who are different from them.

I put my phone down. I have to stay focused on what I need to do today—insulating my science shed—and put this kind of stuff to the back of my mind. And so I abandon my inbox and my tea and get to work. I put on some music and my white-rimmed sunglasses and begin moving stuff out of the shed to make room for us to install the insulation. Iggy goes back inside to watch from the comfort of the AC (he always likes to disappear when hard work is happening, lazy pup). A while later Rebekah comes out and we really get started.

But my thoughts keep floating back to this latest mess with AES and my potential election to the board. Would I be wasting my time if AES doesn't want to change? Should I find another professional society altogether, rather than stick it out here? My experience with AES feels like a microcosm of what happens in the larger world with white supremacy and the patriarchy: white men do whatever they want, and the rules are for *other* people. Then people like me "fight back" while adhering to the rules that were created to keep us in check, while the white man who doesn't think they apply to him openly flouts them. *Yes, you need to ask for permission to apply for a grant. No, I do not.* Which is why I don't believe in following rules that are dumb. And I have always been this way, since childhood. Even at school, once I decided a rule was stupid, I was not going to follow it. And I would accept any consequences for not following it. A rule that applies only to some isn't a rule; it's a manipulation tool.

Everyone should be part of designing the rules and the process. Only when everyone is a part of the process can you create systems that are equitable and fair. If you start making rules about people who aren't sitting at the table, those people will always get the short end of the stick. That's how that works.

. . .

On the military bases where I lived as a kid, I don't ever remember feeling like the odd one out, or different from anyone else. Everyone was from somewhere else and we were all thrown in together. But in 2003, my mother retired from the air force, and we settled in Columbia, not too far from my father's family in Myrtle Beach. When I started sixth grade there, I experienced a true culture shock. During legal segregation, the middle school had been a Black school, and nearly fifty years after *Brown v. Board of Education,* it was still almost entirely made up of Black and Latino students, except for the two magnet programs that were placed in the school to draw wealthy white families out of private schools to balance out its demographics. Due to my good grades, I found myself in one of these magnet programs, bright-eyed and bushy-haired, ready to start middle school.

I was uneasy even before my first day. My parents and I went to an orientation session, and I distinctly remember the person leading the presentation emphasizing, repeatedly, that *all* of our classes would just be with "students in the program." The presenter was trying to address some fear that my child brain didn't understand. She kept repeating that *all* of the classes and magnet student lockers were on their own side of the hall.

I remember a lot of questions from white parents that basically all amounted to, "Will my child have to interact with the 'other students'?" I didn't know why this made me uneasy, but it did.

Then my first day arrived. I felt like a big kid at that new school with my own locker, but when I walked through the door on the magnet-program side of the hallway, a white teacher immediately stopped me.

"Are you lost?" she asked.

I showed her my schedule and told her I didn't think so. *Why had she asked me that?* Then I headed into my homeroom ready to learn, with no idea of what was about to hit me. As I walked into the room, I saw twenty other faces looking back at me, and none of them looked like mine. It was a feeling I had never experienced before. Nonetheless, I shrugged it off, just like I had the teacher's question, and went about my day trying to make friends by sharing school supplies and talking about cartoons.

I realized two things pretty quickly on that day. The first was that a lot of these kids already knew one another: they had gone to the same private schools, lived in the same neighborhoods, played on the same soccer teams, and belonged to the same country clubs. *That's fine,* I remember thinking. How many times had I moved in the middle of a school year and had to wiggle my way into preexisting friend groups? *I can do this.* The second realization was that we didn't speak the same language. Sure, we were all speaking English, but we were not on the same page. They were talking about soccer and cotillion—a word that, admittedly, at the time of writing this, I had to ask my white roommate for, because it still exists only peripherally in my vocabulary—and Abercrombie and American Eagle. I wasn't sure how to join in on conversations I didn't understand. I have the distinct memory of asking someone if their club team was called "Hilfiger" (which I pronounced incorrectly) because they both had it on their shirts. They snickered and I remember thinking, *Okay, I'm done trying to find a way to join this conversation.*

At least I had my homeroom and science teacher, Mr. Compton. I could tell from the moment he walked into the room wearing a caveman costume that he was going to be my favorite teacher. He was a big guy and looked jolly in a one-piece Fred Flintstone outfit while introducing the curriculum on the history of civilization from the cavemen to the present, and the concept of prehistoric paleontology. Mr. Compton is largely the reason I didn't turn around and walk out that door to quit that magnet program on day one. He made us laugh and he made *all* of us the center of attention in his classroom. It's simultaneously fitting and ironic that it was a science teacher who made me feel like I belonged in the magnet program. It's ironic because there have been so many science spaces since then where I have been made to feel I had no place. But Mr. Compton was special. When he died only a few years later of a heart attack, hundreds of his former students turned out for his funeral; he meant so much to so many.

The worst moment of all on that first day of middle school came at lunchtime: walking into the lunchroom and seeing the mostly white faces of my magnet-program classmates on one side of the cafeteria—and everyone who looked like me on the other. Here was my dilemma: I didn't know anyone. I recognized some of my classmates but hadn't connected with them yet. There were people whom I likely could relate to more easily on the other side of the cafeteria—the "other students"—but the magnet program kept us so isolated I hadn't had a chance to meet them. So I did what I do best: I panicked. I just camped out in the bathroom until lunch ended.

When I told my mom about my day and the strangeness of the cafeteria, she gave me some advice that I've continued to carry with me: "Make a new table."

So the next day, I got my food from the cafeteria and sat in what amounted to no-man's-land, a strip of empty tables in the dead center of the cafeteria. I sat there by myself at first, thinking, *Okay, Mom, I don't know if this is better than the bathroom.* Then something happened. Two or three of the other Black girls in the magnet program (which was sadly most of the Black people in the magnet program) joined me at this other table. I was so relieved. I didn't want to sit at that table by myself! Looking back on it, I'm sure they'd had similar experiences to me trying to fit in. I like to imagine that they felt a sense of relief and opportunity when I sat in no-man's-land and offered an alternative.

As the school year went by, more and more people (from both sides of the cafeteria) started joining us. At some point, our group expanded past the one table to a second. By the end of eighth grade, all three tables in that dead zone were filled. Did I change the world? No. The classes were still separate, and the majority of the cafeteria remained segregated, but I learned so much at that little table. I learned that just because something is one way doesn't mean it's the right way, and it doesn't mean it can't change. I learned that you don't need to change the world—you just need to change your small piece of the world. I learned that you can create your own comfort in uncomfortable situations, and, in doing so, create community, create longed-for camaraderie. I learned that I could create a space for me and others like me to belong.

6

On the *Disconnected*
Terra Ceia Bay, Florida

The first shark we catch this morning in Terra Ceia Bay is a very angry, very pregnant bull shark. She whips her tail with amazing force, desperately trying to propel herself out of our grip. I cannot get hold of her tail, and we struggle to pull her into position along the side of the boat. She's girthy— just from looking at her we can see she's carrying pups. With one big, massive jerk, she straightens the big ol' hook and releases herself. In a flash, she is back in the water, gliding away from us.

I lean against the edge of Tonya's boat, the *Disconnected*, speechless. This bull shark's relentless intensity is not normal.

"Looks like she had other ideas," I say. I'm impressed. #Respect.

"Bet she's off to drop those pups right now," Tonya says.

Tonya is my main fishing partner, and her whole vibe is bad*ss. She's the head of the Smalltooth Sawfish Recovery Implementation Team, a group that has been tasked with stewarding the conservation efforts of sawfish in the United States ever since they became listed under the Endangered

Species Act in 2003, and she runs Havenworth Coastal Conservation, her own nonprofit, which conducts research as well as doing a lot of outreach and science education to promote conservation efforts.

Tonya grew up in Grand Haven, Michigan, and Fort Worth, Texas, which is a long way from any salt water—but, like me, she used to go on family vacations to the beach. That's where she fell in love with the ocean, fishing with her dad. When she was about seven years old, she caught her first blacktip, and after that, all she wanted was to be out on the water—or swimming or snorkeling through it. In high school, she wrote reports on the Gulf of Mexico and the marine life there. She read books, watched documentaries, essentially educated herself in everything to do with marine life. After joining the navy, she earned a degree in marine fisheries from Texas A&M. Tonya's someone who never went to graduate school, but she knows her intelligence, she believes in her drive and ability to make significant contributions, and so, without the classic scientist pedigree, she's made a career for herself, rejecting other people's low expectations of her as someone from small towns and without much money, an advanced degree, or (let's be honest) a penis.

For me, Tonya is the *original* rogue scientist. The first time I met her I was in graduate school, doing a sawfish survey in the Everglades. Afterward, we were sitting in the back of a pickup truck heading home for the day, talking loudly over the wind, and I blurted out, "I want to be like you—please let me be your mini-me!" She laughed, and the rest is history. When I left graduate school a couple of years later, not knowing what was next for me, just positive I needed to get out of the toxic academic environment, the one thing I was sure of was that I was going to Tampa Bay, where Tonya was. This lady has shark energy—she's not going to mess with you, but she will bite if necessary.

Today, out on the boat, we're hosting four early-career MISS folks: Jahnita, Jade, Karson, and Naomi—our Eugenie Clark fellows. This is a new fellowship that we named after the one and only Dr. Eugenie Clark, otherwise known as the Shark Lady, a total rebel and one of the very first shark researchers. Genie, as she was known, died in 2015, and in my view, she should be a household name by now—but of course, because she was a woman, and a woman of Japanese descent, most people haven't heard about her or her legacy.

She was born in New York City in 1922 and spent her childhood visiting the aquarium, where she totally fell in love with underwater life. Little Genie used to hang out at the aquarium listening to the docents give tours until she knew the information by heart. She began giving unofficial tours of her own—and eventually, the aquarium had to hire her as a docent because her tours were so good. In 1942, she managed to obtain a BA in zoology from Hunter College, at a time when a woman entering marine sciences was pretty much unheard of. When she went to do graduate work at Columbia University, however, her application was rejected because the university was worried that she would give up her studies as soon as she had children. Undeterred, she went on to get a master's and a doctorate at NYU.

Before Genie came along, scientists hadn't really been researching sharks or shark behavior. People just assumed that sharks were mindless, that they couldn't learn and didn't have memory recall, but Genie proved that was false. To this day, aquariums use Genie's theories around target training, where sharks learn to come and eat at a specific target. One of Genie's greatest legacies is that she founded the lab that grew into the Mote Marine Laboratory & Aquarium, the marine-research organization currently located in Sarasota, Florida, where I got my first big-girl job. When she founded Mote, Genie made sure the lab had an aquarium attached, so that young people could be introduced to a love of marine science the same way she was.

The first time I heard Genie's name, I was an undergrad, and just knowing that a woman was highly regarded in the field of shark science—was in fact one of the founders of shark science and of the American Elasmobranch Society—was very empowering for me as a woman in a male-dominated field. I didn't know that she was a person of color, though, until 2019, when a biography came out about her and I found out that she was Japanese American. Genie was white-passing, so when I looked at pictures of her, it hadn't been obvious to me. I found it interesting that people didn't talk about that aspect of her life—maybe because people who aren't people of color don't think it's an important fact.

When I really got to know more about Genie, though, was during conversations with Tonya, because Tonya had known her and worked with her at Mote. Over the years, Tonya had had many candid conversations with Genie about being a woman in science, and Tonya has passed on a lot of that to me. By Tonya's account, Genie was a force to be reckoned with scientifically and in the way she stuck to her guns and took up space in shark science. A piece of advice she gave

Tonya when Tonya was dealing with a lot of sexism in the field was to "succeed in spite of them." I love that. That's what I aim to do. I actually think spite is a good motivation, and it's a valid one. I want to prove wrong all of the people who told me that I couldn't succeed.

In keeping with Genie's ethos and life's work, the MISS Eugenie Clark fellowship offers female-identifying students and students of color interested in marine science a full-time, paid summer internship. The program provides research experience, as well as outreach and education experience, since the recipients help us with MISS summer camp and Science at the Sea, two free MISS programs for kids. It's not a coincidence that wealth and access to resources fall along race lines in this country—it's by design, and so *we* have to design our programs to fill that financial gap.

Standing on deck, watching the bull shark swim off, S-curving her way as far from us as she can, my heart is pumping faster than it has in a long time. The power in that shark was amazing.

"That was fun!" I say.

"Whoa . . . you guys really tussled there," Jahnita responds, her eyes wide, taking it all in.

Bull sharks have an amazing ability to adjust to a variable and changing environment, reminding us how astounding sharks are in their capacity to do whatever it takes to thrive in their habitat. Bull sharks don't flourish just in salt water; they can adjust to brackish water in estuaries and fresh water in rivers, too. This doesn't mean that they are going to swim up the Connecticut River and bite you while you're on vacation in Vermont or anything. Never fear! Bull sharks are not swimming up into fresh water to get you—they have other things on their mind. You may be thinking, *Nope. Not buying it. I saw* Jaws! *I know it's based on the true story of a shark swimming up a brackish creek in New Jersey in 1916 and attacking a bunch of unsuspecting people.* Yes, that did and can happen. But it's freakishly rare. More than 75 million people swim in the ocean in the United States every year, and there are, on average, sixteen shark bites a year. By comparison, 4.5 million people get bitten by dogs every year in the United States. Shark attacks in brackish water are so rare that the 1916 incident in New Jersey made for one of the best horror movies of all time.

The beautiful shark that just slipped out of our hands was probably on her way upriver to give birth to her pups and give them a good start to life far away from potential predators. Bull sharks have a rectal gland that can adjust the amounts of internal solutes by releasing a compound called urea to balance with the solutes of the water outside. Whenever there's a semipermeable membrane like skin, water will move to where there is more stuff (in science we refer to this "stuff" as solutes), such as particles, ions, salt, and so forth. So if a shark is in salt water, its body has enough solutes so that water doesn't leave its cells and go to where there are more solutes. (Congratulations—you just relearned a process called osmosis! Remember that one from high school?) But when bull sharks swim into fresh water, they have to adjust their internal solute level to stay in balance, and the rectal gland helps them expel their extra solutes through urea. It's an incredible adaptation.

But bull sharks aren't the main reason we're here today.

Tonya does a lot of work with the smalltooth sawfish, and we're going to do some sawfish surveys. I'll collect samples for the bonnethead project here on the Tampa side, while Kathy continues running things in Biscayne Bay.

The smalltooth sawfish is critically endangered, which means this animal is as bad off as it gets before complete extinction happens. It is another odd fish with a weird-looking head, so it is pretty much irresistible to me. It has a long nose that looks like, well, a saw. The saw, or rostrum, has small teeth along its edges, much like perforations along a chainsaw. These teeth are more like human fingernails than traditional shark teeth; they continuously grow—if they chip, no big deal; they will keep growing—but if a tooth is lost from the root, it won't grow back. A sawfish uses its rostrum for a bunch of reasons, including to hunt for food; the fish cuts through a school of fish and circles back to eat whatever is injured. But sawfish are cautious when they hunt; they don't have an endless supply of regrowing teeth, like other elasmobranchs. One time, I caught a male sawfish and he clearly had gotten into a fight or become tangled up in something because he had *no* teeth on one side—none. He was thin, ragged, and looked a bit like what I'd imagine an old-man sawfish looks like. All I could think as his rostrum peeked out from the water's surface was, *You poor, poor old man; you don't have any teeth.* Without a functioning blade, he was likely having trouble getting the food he needed.

(Although I have a lot of bonnethead qualities, I usually think of myself as more of a sawfish. Low-key, until you mess with me, and then I will cut, cut, cut. Don't worry—I have never actually cut anyone.)

Before the industrial revolution, sawfish were all over the western Atlantic. They spread as far north as North Carolina (maybe even New York), as well as down to Florida, around the Gulf Coast, and past the Yucatán Peninsula as far south as Brazil, and ranged throughout the Caribbean. But today, there are only two known viable populations—one in Florida and the other in the Bahamas. That's it. We call these two locations "lifeboat populations," because smalltooth sawfish are all but extinct except in these two isolated areas. The population in Andros (the biggest Bahamian stronghold) is stable for now, but the government there doesn't enforce as many protections as we do in the United States, so protecting sawfish here in Florida is important.

Tonya has a project funded by the Disney Conservation Fund to learn about how sawfish use the Tampa Bay area. We know from her previous research that Charlotte Harbor on the Gulf Coast is an important nursery for sawfish; and from my previous research—which Dr. Minion tried to scoop— we also know that Cape Canaveral on the Atlantic coast of Florida is important for large juveniles and adult smalltooth sawfish, as are networks of routes around the tip of Florida between these two points. But there is still a lot to learn about where else smalltooth sawfish may go, why they go there, and what they do there. Some days, Tonya's out on her boat doing a fishing survey; other days, she's out canvassing docks and beaches to educate people about sawfish and where to report any sightings. Last year, there were sightings of very young sawfish in the area, which begs the question: Is there a nursery here we do not yet know about?

I'm happy to be out with Tonya again after being away for

a few weeks. I don't think there is any better way to spend time than on the water. Not long after the wily pregnant bull shark gets away from us, we catch a blacknose. As the name implies, this shark has a black smudge on the tip of its nose (scientists are really creative with their names). These are smaller sharks, commonly found in the coastal waters of Terra Ceia Bay.

On the research vessel *Garvin,* Dr. Catherine Macdonald and Amani Webber-Schultz hold a blacknose shark as Jake Jerome draws blood from the animal.

A former lab mate of mine fished with Tonya earlier this summer and, for his research, he's left extra transmitters to put in any blacknose she might catch.

"The size class is right," Tonya says as we get the shark in position. "Wanna do it?"

Since leaving the lab at Florida State University, I have not done a lot of surgeries and I'm happy to get the practice. "Yeah, for sure." Hanging off the side of the boat, with the blacknose in the water and upside down, I make a small incision on the underside of the shark, slide the transmitter in just under the skin, and, with the thick needle, suture him up with a bit of guidance from Tonya, since it's been a while.

Be careful what you wish for! We haul in one blacknose after another, and, by the end of the day, all my muscles are burning from leaning over the side of the boat and doing surgeries. But by the third blacknose, I'm once again making some beautiful and quick sutures. And I am happy the fellows get to see me go through this process—being unsure, receiving guidance, and then getting reacquainted with a skill. It's not everywhere that I feel as comfortable as I do with Tonya, to not have to prove myself, but just to be.

"*Dasyatis americana,*" I hear Tonya shout.

"*Dasyatis* forever," I say, as we pull a southern stingray on board.

Taxonomists are constantly fighting with one another about what to call things, and I say, *Y'all have fun with that.* It was a taxonomist who reclassified stingrays, which were known as *Dasyatis,* as a new genus, *Hypanus,* which is an ugly word; Tonya and I have had *Dasyatis* on all our data sheets for years now. So now, we *do* write *Hypanus,* but for Tonya and me, these stingrays will always be *Dasyatis,* a far more pleasing sound to the ear.

Over the course of the day, we don't manage to catch any sawfish or bonnetheads. Since those are the subjects of our studies, some might assume that this has made the trip a failure, but I don't see it that way. We have hooked a ton of other critters for our MISS fellows to see, learn about, and practice working up. When we're done, we dock the boat just behind Tonya's house; she has the sweetest work-from-home setup

I have ever seen. To me, she's living the dream—she's financially secure and doing what she loves, with people she digs.

．　　．　　．

The first time I learned that marine science was an actual job was the summer of my sophomore year of high school, when I attended a science camp called MarineQuest.

Up until that point, I'd gone to the summer camp our church paid for people to attend. As a kid, I'd often go to church on Sundays with my mom (even though my dad comes from a long line of pastors and undertakers, he's never been big on churchgoing). Around age twelve, I joined the youth choir and I started going to the summer camp with the friends I met there. It was called Camp Cedine and it was in the Tennessee mountains. I still love singing our camp song: "In the mountains, on a hillside, there's a place I loved to go . . . Camp Cedine, hallelujah, place of joy and victory."

Camp Cedine was always a Bible camp in name, but until my final year there I would say it was 90 percent camp, 10 percent Bible; mostly we did activities like animal stockade, where I learned how to take care of animals like chickens, goats, and other livestock; horseback riding, swimming, archery, riflery, and arts and crafts, but there was a gospel choir you could join (which I was all about) and we had chapel at the end of every day. Once the visiting weekly speaker was a rapper, Zion, and instead of the traditional chapel songs in the beginning, he performed gospel rap, and it was like a dance party.

But then a woman I'll call Ms. Holier-Than-Thou became the director, and the camp changed. She was an older church mother—which, if you are familiar with Black Southern church culture, you know what I mean when I say that: the kind who wears a hat, sits at the front, and has lots of thoughts and opinions about everything, but mainly about keeping the old traditions, like dresses needing to be below the knee for women, and men needing to wear a jacket and tie. Before her, there were little rules at Cedine that probably only a Christian camp would have, like you had to wear a one-piece bathing suit that didn't have a lot of cutouts and you couldn't wear anything showing a lot of skin. And rule number nine: boys and girls weren't supposed to make inappropriate physical contact. (I don't remember the other rules, just number nine.) Rule number nine was meant to stop people from holding hands, for example, but we used to shout it out randomly for even the most inane forms of physical contact. Like if while playing basketball, a boy touched me when guarding me or stealing the ball, I'd holler: *"Rule number nine!"* Honestly, we all made a big joke out of it.

Once Ms. Holier-Than-Thou took over, there were definitely more than just nine rules. One time, she separated the boys and girls to have a talk about sex and marriage. From what I could tell, the boys hung out with a male counselor while Ms. Holier-Than-Thou lectured the girls. In short, she told us, Don't have sex before marriage because you owe your husband your virginity: it's a gift for your husband. I remember her saying something like, "You don't want to be like chewed-up gum." And after that, you owe him sex. It wasn't about our safety, emotional or physical, it was about how women are for men, and it's your job not to tempt them and to save yourself for the good ones.

This talk was the opposite of what I was taught at home. My mother was a nurse. She was open and clear, evidence-based: sex shouldn't hurt; it should feel good. If it does hurt, then there could be a problem and go check that out. Be up front with a partner. Communicate: I want to do this, or I don't want to do that. If you're not mature enough to have that conversation with someone, you're not mature enough to have sex. And I knew I wasn't mature enough yet, so I was good. When my mother and some of the other parents heard about the things they had started teaching at Camp Cedine, they were not happy, to say the least. The church I grew up going to isn't what I'd call traditional, and I remember that the next year most parents refused to send their kids to the camp. I'm actually not sure if the church even kept sending kids after that or if Ms. Holier-Than-Thou kept running it. But I was done after that summer.

The following year, I went instead to the MarineQuest science camp at the University of North Carolina (UNC) Wilmington. By then, I knew I loved the water, the ocean, and fishing, and was maybe into science. I found the camp by Googling search terms, and it was expensive, whereas Cedine had been free. So my family saved up for it, and I did some light work for people in the neighborhood to help pay my way.

When I got to MarineQuest, I was beyond excited: we kayaked, we snorkeled; we learned about marshes, water-sheds, all sorts of animals that lived in coastal waters; we built a remote-control underwater vehicle; and we traveled around in these cool, twelve-person vans. The counselors were graduate students at UNC Wilmington, and they just really enjoyed the campers and seemed to want to support us and encourage our curiosity. Aside from Mr. Compton, I hadn't experienced anything like this in school. And it felt really good. As a kid, I knew about the existence of about a handful of jobs: lawyer, engineer, doctor, nurse, police officer, veterinarian, electrician, brick mason, landscaper, taxi driver, garbage collector. These were jobs that I saw on TV or in my everyday life, but these camp counselors were getting advanced degrees for real jobs in marine science. I learned that you could actually get paid to study things that lived in the ocean.

MarineQuest opened up the world of science as a future for me. Science is all about following your curiosity. That's what I love about it: it's a systematic way of asking questions and figuring out the answers, and that's it. But science, like faith, can be used as a tool of manipulation and oppression. A common misconception about evolution, a perversion that probably has roots in racist ideology, is that because of natural selection and survival of the fittest, everything that exists now is its best version. Therefore, because superior beings survive and thrive, passing their genes on to the next generation, it follows that inferior ones wither and die. According to this twisting of the truth, humanity and all living things are moving toward an ideal, which implies a hierarchy, with some people or species landing at the top due to some intrinsic moral value; this is where the concept of eugenics or racial superiority comes in. And while it's true that natural selection allows for some genes that are better adapted to the environment to be passed on and others to die out, there is more to the story.

Environments and situations can change, sometimes rapidly. What may be a benefit in one situation might be a hindrance in another. Natural selection isn't the only mechanism that drives evolution. Genetic drift is another—this occurs when just by chance a selection of the population gets taken out by a random event. Imagine there are a bunch of lizards, and some have red spots and some have yellow ones. They all live on an island where suddenly a volcano erupts. Let's say that most of the lizards die (this would be what we'd call a mass extinction event), but maybe five red-spotted lizards survive because they happened to be in a cave when the volcano erupted and they were protected from the lava. Suddenly, there are no more yellow-spotted lizards, not because red-spotted lizards were better adapted but because the few lizards that survived just so happened to have red spots. The color of the spots didn't help or hurt the lizards, and neither lizard was "better" than the other.

Mutation is another mechanism for evolution. Sometimes our genes (portions of our DNA that control different traits) just mutate. This process is also random. Maybe one day a lizard is born with a tooth on its tail (this is perhaps a silly example, but stay with me). Sometimes we tend to think of mutations as bad things, but mutations are just a variation. That variation may be helpful in some situations, detrimental in others—or it might not affect anything at all. Maybe the tooth on the lizard's tail makes it too heavy to, say, climb a tree and get the fruit it needs to eat, in which case it would die and never pass on its mutation. However, let's say our tail-toothed lizard figures out how to crack open bird eggs by hitting them with its tail, and it gets tons of protein from them. Now our toothy lizard lives a long, healthy life and has lots of babies—and its babies live a long time and have lots of babies—and eventually there are a bunch of lizards running around with teeth on their tails. Sure, this mutation changed the way they got food, but they were still able to get it. Having a tooth is fine, not having a tooth is fine: no matter what, you're able to thrive.

In fact, for the lizards this variation could be a good thing. Let's say suddenly the environment changes and that fruit the tooth-free-tailed lizards have depended on vanishes. These lizards start dying, but the tooth-tailed lizards aren't impacted by this, so the species is able to continue on, thanks to the variation. That's what people who practice eugenics fail to see. If you make everyone the same, you are all susceptible to the same things. The chances of you encountering something no one in the group can handle decreases when there is more variation. It's the reason that scientists always talk so much about the importance of biodiversity and economists talk about diversifying your portfolio, and it's the reason behind the saying "Don't put all your eggs in one basket."

The ironic thing is that, although the science community recognizes the value of biodiversity, they are still *very* slow on the uptake when it comes to realizing that this concept applies to them as well. When you have a homogeneous group of people (in this case, scientists) addressing problems or questions and experimenting with answers and solutions, your chances of someone having the right combination of knowledge, skills, and background increase as your workforce diversity increases. That's why at MISS we say, "Diversity in scientists leads to diversity in thought, which leads to innovation." So there is a scientific reason that we need diversity, but there are many other moral reasons as well.

Humans are complex in ways that lizards, tooth-tailed or untoothed, are not; I believe we have a soul (or mind or sentience or whatever you want to call it) that is separate from our body. It makes us who we are. And the complexity of humans, so different from all other animals on earth, means that we crave more than mere survival. We need more than just food, water, shelter, warmth. We need understanding, safety, control, meaning, and community. Excluding people from a community, putting them in situations where they don't feel safe or supported, means you are cutting them off from their emotional needs. People can survive and not live. The living comes from engaging together in community. The living comes from feeling safe, valued, and welcome.

Having an equitable and inclusive science field and society as a whole ensures that no one feels excluded, unsafe, undervalued, or unwelcome. Even if there weren't an evolutionary or scientifically proven benefit to diversity, it would still be important because our sentience means that we have an ability to care beyond what makes sense for the good of the group. It means we can feel empathy and recognize that people, regardless of their background, deserve to live and experience the things that interest them, not simply just survive.

I don't know about you, but I want to do more than just survive. I want to live. I want my life to have purpose and meaning. I want to leave the world better than I found it.

Science is a tool that I use to achieve this, but my life is not just science. All these other parts of my identity don't take away from my ability to do science, they add to it. The science community often tries to get people to leave the rest of who they are at the door, but we should be encouraging them to bring it all with them, because that diversity of experiences they have lived is valuable.

I came home after the MarineQuest camp and told my parents that I wanted to be a marine scientist. But as much as they fully supported my dreams, when I wanted to go back to MarineQuest the following year, it just wasn't possible. The cost was too high and we couldn't make it work, so I never returned. Today, almost every aspect of MISS camp is based on my experience at MarineQuest, where I learned so much. The one major difference: MISS camp is free for everyone.

7

At Reddington and Madeira Beaches
St. Petersburg, Florida

The ideal places for baby sawfish to thrive are by mangrove trees and forests. The juvenile fish like to go up into the prop roots of red mangroves to hide and avoid predators: the underwater roots create a protective cover. Perhaps the worst place for a baby sawfish is a public beach. It's open, exposed, and beachgoers often try to handle the critters, as they are so tiny. Adult sawfish grow into big, strong apex predators, up to four and a half meters long, but newborns are small enough to hold with two hands. Sawfish are now so endangered that researchers need permits to touch them, but last year we were seeing pictures pop up on social media of little baby sawfish along a strip of public beaches in St. Petersburg, on the southeastern curve of the Gulf.

Today, Tonya and I are at that strip of coastline that includes Reddington, Madeira, and other beaches, to see if any baby sawfish are back this summer. Our working theory about last year's sightings is that a mama sawfish, en route to somewhere that was definitely not here at this public beach, stress-pupped, which means she gave birth prematurely due to stress; perhaps she was caught by a fisherman. There was also a wastewater disaster at Piney Point in Tampa Bay last year, and the mother may have abandoned her intended pupping site after sensing poor water quality. Regardless of the reason, those pups ended up on the beach. We don't really expect that mama sawfish to be back this summer because (1) this was never her intended location, so she would go somewhere else if she could help it; and (2) if, for some reason that we could never fathom, this horrible place *was* her intended destination, sawfish pup every other year, and so she wouldn't be giving birth this year anyway. We hope and expect that there will be no vulnerable baby sawfish here, but they also never should have been here last year, so we're double-checking.

Juvenile sawfish like very shallow water, so instead of doing our survey on the *Disconnected*, we'll walk the beach and wade into the shallows. We have a simple, handheld net and will be able to measure and tag the animals on the spot. The row of public beaches extends maybe six to seven miles along the coastline, so we decided it might be fun to bike it instead of walking.

"Well, this was a terrible idea," I say, dropping my rented bike. The tide was high this morning and there's no firm ground for a bike, just soft sand. My thighs burn like crazy, and no matter how hard I push, the bike fights me. "Are you dying, 'cause I'm dying," I tell Tonya.

"Yeah, this sucks!" Tonya says. She's lugging around our nets to help haul in anything we may see, cameras to document everything, tagging equipment for any sawfish we may catch, and a stack of educational flyers to inform the public about these critically endangered animals. She uses a small child's wagon to lug it all, and it's more than forty pounds of stuff. She's a shade of bright red I haven't seen before. She throws her bike onto the sand. "I'm over it."

We lock up the rental bikes and hit the beach on foot, after all.

I feel the morning breeze on the back of my neck as we walk silently for a bit. We keep our eyes locked on the water as it sparkles. A few miles into our walk, I think maybe I see something. It is a dark, vaguely sawfish-shaped shadow undulating in the water and it's the right length. I walk closer, the warm water splashing my ankles: the shape looks like it's wiggling around a bit.

With a handheld net on a smalltooth sawfish patrol

"Hey!" I tell Tonya. "Hold on a sec." I do the stingray shuffle gently through the surf, dragging my feet to alert any lurking stingrays so I don't end up with a barb in my leg. I feel my heart lurch, some affection and joy, until, *nope*.

"Just algae," I call out to Tonya, who is on the dry sand with the cart. I dejectedly walk out of the surf.

We continue our trek. Two older women out for what looks like their morning walk are coming toward us.

"Please keep an eye out for sawfish," Tonya says, stretching her hand out to offer them our educational flyer.

They both smile, one taking the flyer, while keeping their brisk pace.

"Will do!" they say in unison.

They've seen these flyers many times before, probably. Tonya posts them at every dock, every beach, anywhere people might come into contact with the elusive sawfish. #Don'tTouch. #Call-1-844-4Sawfish. If you're thinking that's one too many numbers, you are correct. Fun fact: phones ignore the extra digit and send the caller to the hotline all the same, and, just like an infomercial jingle, the number Tonya came up with makes it easier to remember.

As we walk, I wonder about where that mama sawfish from last year could have been going. The juveniles that we saw on social media, and which Tonya saw some of in person last year, were too small to have made the trip from Charlotte Harbor, the closest known nursery.

"Man, I wish we knew where that mama had been planning on pupping," I say.

"Wouldn't that be nice?" Tonya agrees.

There are only so many places I can think of. Mangroves, which are so important to fish nurseries, are disappearing for a handful of reasons. With rising water temperatures at this latitude, it has become too warm for mangroves to thrive like they used to. The trees seem to be migrating north, and perhaps sawfish populations will follow, but we'll have to wait and see. Mangroves also need a lot of fresh water to grow—

fresh water that rains down from the sky onto mountaintops and flows back to the ocean via our rivers and tributaries. But more and more, all the water is getting used up before it reaches the end of that line, the coast, for mangrove forests. We humans are using it all, rerouting the water with dams and hydraulic controls to distribute water to this or that area/state/city in such a way that some places are left thirstier than others. (Just as an aside, Google *"Arizona v. California"* to dip into the politics and the complicated issues around water distribution for wealthier and less-wealthy states. All I'll say, once again, is that there is enough water for all of us, but there is not enough water for all of us if we let some people be greedy while leaving others without; water, like any resource, needs to be distributed more equitably.) And, of course, mangroves are also under threat by human development—waterfront property owners who tend to cut the trees back or eliminate them entirely because they want a view, a place to dock their boats, and so on.

The loss of these healthy, viable nursery habitats is an ongoing problem. So long as temperatures rise faster than animals can adapt, we will see the wisdom of nature disrupted in ways we don't yet understand. Last year, the morning after Tonya tagged some of the Madeira Beach pups, the sea-turtle patrol found one of them washed up dead. I was home getting dressed to head out to the beach with her to look for more when she called me, crying.

"It was not a safe place for them. I wanted to move them," she said, sobbing. "I should have just *moved them.*"

I began to cry with her, frustration overcoming me. I felt like I could hear her thoughts: *Are we helping? Is any of this helping these animals in a meaningful way?* For a few weeks after that, we walked the beach looking for the other pup she'd tagged or more babies from the same litter. But we didn't see any.

I wonder if that might be my next research project. Maybe after the bonnethead project, I can try to figure out where Mama Sawfish was intending to go. Is nearby Tampa Bay potentially important for this endangered animal we're trying to revive? I feel confident I could get some funding to research that very important scientific question, but I put it on the back burner for now.

Ahead of us on the beach, a bunch of people are looking at something in the water. I grab the camera, Tonya takes a net, and we leave the cart behind. A little farther out than knee-deep we come upon a school of cownose rays. There must be about forty of them gliding majestically through the water. Their snouts are flat and mushed, like the nose of a cow, and they are swimming all around me. I film them for a bit; maybe I can use the footage for a school event for kids, a booth at a conference, or social media—it's a happy scene to remind folks how amazing marine life is.

Unlike sawfish, cownose rays are still plentiful. While their shallow coastal habitats are under threat from pollution, they are not overfished or threatened the way sawfish are. The sawfish's rostrum makes it really vulnerable to big commercial nets. Some studies have shown that sharks and rays, such as the sawfish, have pretty small hearts compared to the size of their bodies, and so when they get twisted in nets and their bloodstream starts to fill with their stress hormone, lactate, they are not able to metabolize it the way, for example, humans can metabolize cortisol when we take deep breaths or stand with our arms over our heads after a big race. So as time passes in stressful situations, the lactate continues to fill their cells until it's just too much, and they literally die of stress.

As expected, Tonya and I didn't see any little sawfish on Reddington or Madeira Beach. And I wonder about them—are they really not here, or are they here just watching me do my silly stingray shuffle and laughing at me, like, "Nah, we're not messing with that human."

Walking the beach with Tonya Wiley, looking for juvenile smalltooth sawfish

As we walk quietly, I start to imagine that the baby sawfish Tonya tagged last year is still alive. I picture that sawfish in a mangrove shoreline somewhere, where she is living comfortably. Sammy, I'll call her. Sammy the sawfish. I imagine her nestling underneath the mangrove prop roots to hide from nocturnal predators like hungry lemon sharks and grumpy bull sharks. Baby sawfish are not very fast compared to other marine species. Sammy'll never outswim a predator like a lemon shark, so she needs to stay low, protected.

When the tide is about to change, Sammy swims out to look for food. She heads to the mouth of an intertidal creek just when the tide is going out and all the fish are moving. She sits at the mouth, where she knows the fish are going to be coming through. And when the moment is right, she'll go slash slash slash slash, and whip her rostrum into a school of fish, then circle back to swallow the ones she's injured. After that she will probably find a nice comfy place and rest on the seafloor for a while. If Sammy the sawfish lives and grows to be bigger than two meters, say in five years' time, she may

Standing next to a large juvenile smalltooth sawfish during a workup in the Florida Keys

start making the migration down the Gulf Coast of Florida through Tampa Bay and Egmont Channel, toward the Florida Keys, and maybe, just maybe, we'll pick up her signal on a receiver. That's my hope. Maybe I'll see her again when she's grown into a teenager. Maybe we'll even catch her in a survey. I wonder what exciting stories she'll have to tell about growing up.

.   .   .

My teenage years were tumultuous. I initially went to the magnet program at Spring Valley High School, following my STEM track from middle school, but it wasn't meant to be. Spring Valley was the wealthiest school in our district by a long shot, located between two well-off neighborhoods that were largely white. Many of the kids who went there were not only white but also wildly, absurdly wealthy. Each morning, in the school parking lot, I'd drive past the row of somewhat-to-be-expected Hondas, Nissans, Toyotas. Then, I'd hit a row with Ferraris, BMWs, Jaguars, and Range Rovers. ("Why on earth are *children* driving BMWs and Range Rovers?" my mother asked one day when she dropped me off.) And, finally, in the very back, was the row with mostly pickup trucks belonging to the kids in camo. Even at prom, these kids wore camo tuxedos. They tried hard to seem like just country boys, going muddin' (which is driving big trucks through the mud), but these kids were just as wealthy as the Jaguar kids. Their trucks were big, and lifted, and expensive. They would blast rap music and fly the Confederate flag off the back. They confused the heck outta me.

The magnet program was filled with kids competing with everyone else to get perfect grades. It was a place that required you to take the hardest version of any class and to perform an unrelenting push to do your best, every day. No—do better than your best! Go beyond what you think you can do! Give it 110 percent! But that is literally not possible. I have only 100 percent. And there was so much more I wanted to do in high school. I loved basketball, theater, Latin dance club, and, because I was a nerd, my classes, too. I tried to pack it all in. On opening night of the play, sophomore year, we also had a basketball scrimmage. The coach complained to my parents, telling them to get me to quit theater, since the basketball program at Spring Valley was, like everything at Spring Valley, very competitive, intense, and focused on being the best. Instead, I showed up to the game in full theatrical hair and makeup, wearing my jersey, but not available to actually go on court—and then ran off to do the play.

At Spring Valley, I attempted to give 100 percent, 100 percent of the time, but soon I was running on empty. When things feel like too much for me, and I feel as if I'm in the wrong environment, my anxiety can get overwhelming, and during that year of high school, it began to flare intensely. I woke up some mornings sick to my stomach. I was so stressed, I started to sleepwalk, fumbling around the house and into my parents' room, talking about a big test I had coming up.

I've always been prone to anxiety. The first panic attack I had was in kindergarten, when we were living in Texas—and it's probably where the claustrophobia started that has plagued me my whole life. A kid in my class was upset about something and he got into one of the little half-lockers we all had and was sitting there crying. Then everyone in class decided to try to fit in the lockers, and five-year-old Jasmin decided to take it a step further and climbed in and closed the door. Of course, I couldn't open the locker from the inside. Suddenly, a gloom washed over me: I knew I had made a grave error. I started yelling for help but I panicked so much, I blacked out. I don't remember anything else—not how long I was in there, or how I got out. After that, whenever I feel super stressed or confined, I experience that same gloom coming over me, then the uncontrollable sense of panic rising. And in high school, I was experiencing this feeling on a daily basis.

So I decided to quit the magnet program. A lot of people have negative feelings about the idea of quitting: they believe you should never give up, even if you want to. But I truly feel like the world would be a much better place if more people simply quit what did not serve them, leaving space for what did matter, even if it looked less prestigious or impressive to others.

Ironically, the way it went down began with the program coordinator calling me into her office to tell me how well I was doing; she told me what a strong student I was. I didn't have a vocabulary for it yet, but I intuitively knew I would burn out if I didn't quit, so I told her that I wanted to leave. She didn't understand that I might want to leave voluntarily. She seemed to think the only reason I would exit a top-tier program would be if I was failing academically. But I was thriving academically and therefore, in her mind, obviously could handle it—at least outwardly. No questions were asked about my mental health or experience. She didn't understand.

She called my mother.

"Why do I need to come in?" my mother asked. She hates being called at work. If you are calling my mom, a nurse, at work, you better be dying; there better be blood. "I understand my daughter would like to leave the program. Why do I need to come in?"

"To sign the paperwork," the project coordinator said.

So a week later, my mother left work two hours early to come to the school.

"Okay, what do I need to sign?" my mother said.

The head of the program began to explain to my mother how well I was doing, how there was no need and no reason for me to leave a program that was as highly regarded and ranked as the magnet program at Spring Valley. But my mother doesn't take well to being told things she already knows as if she doesn't already know them, and she didn't appreciate the fact that no one at the school had asked a single question about why I wanted to leave. When she is upset, my mom talks with a sugary, sweet cadence, akin to "bless your heart," with a smile that tells you, "You f***ed up."

Mom sat up straighter, and I knew what was coming. I kept my mouth shut and just watched.

"Well, it sounds like my daughter has made her decision. I'm only here to sign the paper y'all told me to come in and sign."

Smile.

"We want to be sure that Jasmin has thought this out. Graduating from this program would look really good on her college applications."

"I'm sure she's considered that," my mom said with undertones of, *So what does it tell you that she wants to leave? Is there any reflection that you are not serving my child? Any capacity to understand how she feels as a Black girl in this highly competitive, all-white, wealthy place?* "Show me where I need to sign."

My mom and my dad have always had different styles of navigating the world. From them, I learned when to go high and when to go low, how to use all of the tools at my disposal, adapt however was necessary, and to keep going with self-respect intact, even when it was scary or hard. While I tend to replicate my dad's blunt and direct way of fighting back, my mom prefers the subtle long game that no one sees coming. She hints at the tip of the iceberg with a smile on her face, and the icy coldness in her eyes speaks volumes about what may be below the surface. The one thing that my parents have in common? An unwavering belief in me and my abilities. It's on this that they are in lockstep, for which I am forever grateful.

That day in the school office, my mother quickly scribbled her name and gave the coordinator a cutting and final *So I guess we're done here* look. I nodded my goodbye, and we walked out.

I still took AP and honors classes at Spring Valley, but not all the ones required for the magnet program. That freed up my schedule to do theater—to direct and also perform in every production each year. Ms. McNealy, the theater teacher, was the best. And I hung out in classes that interested me, even though I wasn't enrolled. My senior year, when I was set to take AP Spanish, it wasn't offered, so I just hung out with Señora Ham during free periods, and she would teach me some of the things that I would've learned in the class. I was a big nerd and a teacher's pet (and darn proud of it). I enjoyed hanging out in AP American History, even though I wasn't enrolled, because Mr. Adler was so funny. I took the tests and quizzes, just for funsies, because I was there so often. When he shared the test results, he shared mine, too (with my permission), saying, "And this is what Jasmin—who isn't even actually taking this class—scored. Do with that information what you will."

Mr. Smoak was a favorite as well. What really sold me on him was what happened one day, after college acceptances had come in, when I noticed that a girl in our honors statistics class, who I'll call Nosy Nancy, was in a particular huff.

"Well," she said, for everyone in the class to hear, "I sure wish I was a minority so that I could get into Duke."

Keep in mind I had gotten into Duke, and an Asian boy named Han had, too. There were two white kids in the class who had applied as well but had not been accepted—Nancy and a boy named Jamie. Mr. Smoak looked right at me, and then turned around toward the whiteboard, as if to say, *If you hit her right now, I didn't see it.*

But Jamie got there first. "No, Nancy," he said. "Jasmin got into Duke and I didn't because Jasmin had a better application." And he practically rolled his eyes out of his own head at her.

"Well," she said, moving on, "we know everyone's ranking in this class but nine and ten." She had been trying to piece together the class rankings because the top ten were the ones who got to sit onstage at graduation. "C'mon, who is nine and ten?"

Jamie leaned over to me and whispered, "I'm number ten. I'm just not going to tell her because she's annoying."

"I'm number nine," I whispered back, "and I'm not going to tell her, either."

"I kind of figured that," he replied.

She looked over at the two of us, then away.

"If you're not telling, it's probably because you are not at the top, and you're embarrassed," she insisted.

Another glance my way.

"I have nothing to be embarrassed about, Nancy," I said.

It was super delightful, then, to see her face at graduation rehearsal later that month. I was onstage, already seated, when she arrived in the auditorium.

I turned and gave her a smile.

No way, her expression seemed to say.

I smiled back. *Yup!*

Nancy's someone that I'd guess probably got some satisfaction from the fact that, despite having gotten in, I actually couldn't afford to go to Duke. Who knows? After high school, she went off to Clemson, and I went on a scholarship to the College of Charleston, where I ended up having the time of my life.

If I had stayed in the magnet program, if I had given up theater and things that I loved to take classes that someone else was telling me I should take, I would most certainly have burned out. Every time I have decided to step off my current or expected path and take a different route, it has served me well. Just because you start down one road doesn't mean you have to keep going down it if it no longer fills you up.

8

At Home
Tampa, Florida

The loss of viable habitats is a huge stress on sawfish, but perhaps the biggest threat for them is commercial fishermen accidentally scooping them up when they are trying to fish for other things (which usually leads to the sawfish dying). We call the accidental catching of a nontarget species "bycatch." Shrimp trawl fisheries, for example, use huge nets that they drag for long distances before being hauled in. The sawfish rostrum is easily tangled in their nets, and the longer they thrash in these nets, the more sawfish can get themselves all kinds of twisted up.

Commercial fishing bycatch is also one of the least studied and understood threats to smalltooth sawfish. The first step to helping a species listed under the Endangered Species Act is identifying places that are important for their recovery and designating them as "critical habitats," which is a legal term that mandates that certain protections be applied to those areas. Critical habitats have been established for juvenile smalltooth sawfish in each of their known nursery areas. But once they grow beyond two meters and start to leave these protected places, what happens? Where do they go? Do they need further protection? When I was in graduate school, my team and I worked to fill this data hole. We tagged forty-three sawfish that were longer than two meters, using acoustic transmitters with five- or ten-year battery lives to track their movements. We combined our findings with that of other sawfish researchers as members of groups called iTAG and FACT and amassed a huge dataset.

Acoustic transmitters emit sounds that are picked up by receivers, which are very expensive and difficult to maintain. One research program may have a handful of receivers, but of course animals swim all over, in and out of range of a particular program's receiver. So iTAG and FACT were formed to foster collaboration between scientists for the sake of science. The basic agreement is this: if you pick up my tag on your receiver, give it to me, and I will do likewise. In this way, we can each track the specific animals that we tagged for our individual projects up and down the southern Atlantic coast of the United States and the Bahamas. To avoid any confusion about who owns what, all participants are required to sign a contract that says the person who tagged the animal is the one who owns the data. So when you get detections on your receiver for tags that don't belong to you, you upload the data from your receiver to a database that we all share.

Over several years of collecting data that pinged on a huge network of receivers, we were able to learn where they went. And the results were encouraging: sawfish were traveling farther north than scientists previously thought, and, if this trend continued, it meant they were on their way to returning to their previous range. Hope was on the horizon!

Dr. Minion's program had a receiver, and he was part of this collective group. When he unethically manipulated the system to take my data, which had showed up on his receiver, he made exaggerated claims that the area around his receiver was potentially a critical habitat for sawfish. That is a big claim, a rock-star claim—if accurate—with major economic repercussions. Overstating the importance of an area for an endangered species can have potentially devastating impacts for folks who rely on certain goods and services from those areas. Scientists, policymakers, and resource managers have to be careful when making claims and recommendations. Given the wealth of data we had for our study looking at which areas are important for sawfish, we felt that more research was required to make a critical habitat claim and that Minion was overstating the importance of the area around his receiver.

So I refuted Minion's overstated claim, and in a follow-up paper, I calculated the risk of sawfish bycatch in some areas my first paper identified as important. The paper recommended a time-area closure, which is closing a designated area of importance for a limited period of time when risk of bycatch is highest. This recommendation was essentially the opposite of what regulators were considering at the time, which was easing the restrictions on the fisheries by increasing the number of sawfish that could be caught as bycatch before the fishery was shut down.

The possibility of easing protections for sawfish just as we were beginning to reap the benefits of those protections was frustrating. A colleague at the National Oceanic and Atmospheric Administration (NOAA) presented my paper to the policymakers to encourage them to reconsider easing restrictions. He showed them the places where sawfish spent their time and the rate at which they could be killed in those areas if not protected. The decision to nevertheless ignore the science and ease the restriction was disheartening, but not surprising.

A few months ago, Ginger, a graduate student in marine biology and a MISS member, reached out asking for assistance in finding a project. Her time frame was tight; her adviser had not been a help. I often find myself mentoring MISS members like Ginger, who didn't have an adviser who gave her the time of day, meaning she had to go looking for outside help in order to graduate. I thought it could be great for her to explore possible alternative policy recommendations for my bycatch paper; perhaps she could figure out ways to offer regulators new options that still gave sawfish significant protections but also were more amenable to the shrimp fisheries. All of the data was already collected, so it could fit her tight time frame. A win-win.

Ginger liked the idea, but she didn't know how to use the necessary software programs. I told her, "If you drive down from Jacksonville, I'll teach you everything you need." So today, I am teaching her about a geographic information systems software called QGIS, which would allow her to look at data from different locations and determine when there is the highest chance of overlap and potential bycatch mortalities.

"Where were we?" I say to Ginger, who is sitting at my kitchen table with her laptop open.

"I'm about to download the files you sent onto my C drive," Ginger says. She gently touches the mouse pad, so unsure.

"Great!" I say. "That small step is important. I learned the hard way that if you store things in any folder besides the C drive, if you ever try to open the maps on a different computer, it can't find the data because every computer's folder naming system is different, except for the C drive."

I created the starting map for her before we met up, which integrates a bunch of different raw datasets—satellite data, acoustic data, fishing effort data, and grids of information—that can be downloaded into QGIS, which can then spit out a 2D representation of all of that data. From there, it's a pretty easy visual process of looking at the graphs and determining where there is a lot of overlap.

I sit on the couch in my living room, with Iggy resting his head on my thigh, while I give her some space to work. I read an email from Tonya saying that we'll be able to go out again next week on the *Disconnected* with some MISS folks. And I reply to Kathy, who decided to switch from an internship-based master's to a thesis-based master's; she's enjoyed working on the bonnethead project and it's inspired her to make it her master's thesis. When Tonya and I go out on the *Disconnected* later, I'll be looking to collect bonnethead samples for Kathy's data, as it has evolved into more of her project than mine—she will take on the role of compiling the info and publishing. I don't feel at all possessive; I still get to do the fun stuff. I love being out on the water, helping people collect their data, problem-solving or troubleshooting, and I'm learning how much I love bringing people together to get the work done.

.   .   .

A friend recently asked if I was upset or had feelings about not being able to afford to go to Duke and attending the College of Charleston instead. Would a shark regret that it got its food from feasting on a tilapia instead of the grouper that got away? No, it efficiently digests all the energy from the tilapia and heads back out for the next meal. I'm like a shark; I keep it moving.

I chose the College of Charleston because it had a good marine science program, and after the MarineQuest camp, I knew marine science could be a job. The College of Charleston's marine biology department nourished me in all the ways I could have hoped. It also introduced me to sharks.

Freshman year, I went to a research matchmaking event in the biology department. I circled the event, but everyone I spoke to told me they had no funding for undergraduate research. I was about to leave when a hurricane of a person, looking at something in his hands, burst through the door and collided with me.

"I'm terribly sorry," he said. He had disheveled, silvery hair and a wide smile, and he spoke with a thick accent that I couldn't place—South African, Australian . . . British?

"Oh, no, I'm sorry," I said, stooping to pick up everything that had fallen to the floor. I helped carry his stuff to his booth and we chatted. Turns out he *was* British, although he had been born in Tanzania, where his dad was working as an exploration geologist. His name was Dr. Gavin Naylor, and he was late to set up his booth, which I would learn was very on-brand for him.

When I met him, Gavin was working on the Chondrichthyan Tree of Life Project, a subset of the Tree of Life Project, which aimed to use DNA sequencing to gather the genome of every living thing on earth. Gavin's focus was on chondrichthyans (sharks, skates, rays, and chimaeras). He was building a website where people could access the genome of every shark species and also look at their anatomy using 3D digital models built from CT scans of specimen samples. It was wicked cool! At that point, sharks weren't really on my radar. They were just animals that existed until, by luck, I literally bumped into Gavin.

"Are you interested in helping with my research?" he asked me as we stood by his booth.

I was interested, but having had a series of professors just tell me that they had no funding to pay undergraduate researchers, I tried to keep my expectations in check.

"I'm looking for a funded position," I told him. No matter how much I wanted to do research, I wasn't able to give up my tutoring job for something unpaid.

"I don't have any funding for an undergrad," he said, "but let me see if I can figure something out." We exchanged email addresses.

I walked off that afternoon and didn't think about Gavin until months later, when he emailed me out of the blue: "Hey. Have you heard of the Fort Johnson REU program?" It was a paid internship for undergraduates. I told him I had, but I was only a rising sophomore that summer, and it was for juniors and seniors.

"It's okay," he wrote back. "Just go ahead and apply."

I did and I got it. And that was the summer, as a paid intern, that I got my first shark experience—and it changed my life.

Gavin moved mountains to find me undergraduate funding over the years after that internship. I began to work in his lab. As I got to know him better, I learned that he'd taken a winding path to shark science. Growing up in East Africa, surrounded by incredible wildlife like elephants, giraffes, and wildebeests, he had decided he wanted to be a game ranger, and so he ended up studying zoology at Durham University in England. Later, while he was doing graduate work at the University of Maryland, he met a professor of evolutionary biology named Lin Chao. Dr. Chao introduced him to the wonders of studying evolution, and Gavin was hooked. He started to realize he wanted to find a group of animals he could study to understand more about molecular evolution and how those animals had diversified. He looked at various mammals and mollusks, but those subjects were taken, and eventually his adviser, who was a paleontologist, suggested sharks. Gavin began traveling the world collecting shark specimens, which led to a postdoc in paleontology. How lucky that I happened upon a mentor in academia who was passionate, brilliant, generous, and kind (and who happened to be white and male).

Honoring my good fortune in finding Gavin and having his support, I threw myself into the study of sharks. I decided to take on a project to see if I could use genetic analysis and digital segmentation to make the two rival hammerhead phylogenies agree. Evolutionary biologists try to build family trees to hypothesize how species—including sharks—and their features evolved, and this family tree is called a phylogeny, an attempt to puzzle out the evolutionary history of a group of animals using fossils, tissues, specimens, and so forth. The basic assumption a researcher uses when building a phylogeny is that the more similar the things, the more closely related they are.

Prior to the 1950s, scientists created phylogenies based on the anatomy of an animal, in order to hypothesize how and in what sequence the species evolved. But that changed when a woman named Rosalind Franklin discovered the structure of DNA. (You may have been taught in school that Watson and Crick made this discovery, because, as is often the case, women of note in science are written out of the history books.) Previously, whenever people thought about evolution, they imagined it as a progression toward something optimal—there was an ape who evolved into a bipedal human, who evolved into the upright contemporary man in a suit. But progression implies that evolution is linear (and slow), and it's not. That's an oversimplification. Evolution is more radial. If we think in visual terms, there are many points at which random mutations occur and have a ripple effect that goes through one line of animals. Thanks to Franklin's discovery, genetics offered a new world of information. Instead of assuming that some anatomical feature that's useful and helps an animal survive is the result of a slow progression, researchers learned, for example, that a genetic mutation can create a relatively sudden anatomical change. Plot twist!

For hammerheads, the phylogeny based on the analysis of the DNA contradicts and in fact reverses the long-standing phylogeny based on anatomy. The hypothesis based on anatomy suggests that their heads have been getting larger over time and that the hammerheads that are most closely related to the common ancestor of all the hammerheads are the sharks with small heads, like bonnetheads. Meanwhile, the DNA-based hypothesis suggests that the heads have been getting *smaller* over time and that the hammerhead most closely related to the common ancestor is the shark with the widest head, the winghead shark. If hypothesis number one is correct, it suggests that natural selection has been driving the head wider over time, which would mean it must have some evolutionary advantage; this, in turn, provides evidence that there may be a special role or niche that hammerheads occupy in the marine environment that a shark with a regular head shape might not be able to fulfill. If hypothesis number two is correct, it suggests that the wide head was a random mutation that hasn't been particularly valuable and has been slowly evolving away, which means the hammer likely provides no benefit to the animals. In other words, it's a fluke (bad joke, since a fluke is also a tail). Of course, there is always a third option, which is that neither hypothesis is correct.

Science doesn't (or shouldn't) allow one to simply ignore data that doesn't lead to the conclusions you want or hope to be true; it usually does lead to somewhere unexpected—and far more interesting. Is it time for researchers to update their commonly held assumptions on how to build a phylogeny? If the basic assumption to follow when building a phylogeny is that similar things are more closely related, what do you use for your comparison: the anatomy or the genetics? Often, they tell the same story, but sometimes they don't. One gene can result in a big anatomical difference. Think about hair color in humans. Genetically, the different colors are not that different, but the strawberries-and-cream complexion of one human looks very different from the chocolate complexion of another. Are these different shark heads the result of natural selection or random mutation? Researchers have yet to agree.

For my research project in Gavin's lab, I began with rebuilding both hammerhead phylogenies—one using anatomy and one using genetics—but with one tweak: for the phylogeny based on anatomy, I excluded the head. My reasoning was that the head may be providing a distraction and biasing the data. I was more interested in what the rest of the body had to say. Using CT scans of specimens, I dissected them virtually through a process called digital segmentation and was able to isolate and categorize each piece of anatomy noninvasively. Then I re-created the phylogeny based on an analysis of the DNA, but also with one tweak: instead of using DNA from the nucleus, I took DNA from the mitochondria, which contains DNA passed down only from the mother, not a mix of the mother's and father's; it therefore changes less than DNA in the nucleus. My thinking was that perhaps this DNA would show something lost or convoluted in the mixed DNA. Ultimately, I did not get the phylogenies to agree, but I sussed out what might be the source of the confusion: we've yet to correctly identify the oldest common hammerhead ancestor and therefore we're using the wrong starting point. This is called a rooting problem in evolutionary studies, and until some enterprising, brilliant human figures out how to realign the evolutionary clock, we will never really be able to build an accurate phylogeny.

During those college years, I was in pursuit of a clear goal. It was exciting: I got to learn about almost every aspect of Gavin's lab, which is rare for an undergraduate. I was invited to lab meetings, and I was arguably doing master's-level work. The funding Gavin found for me, when others said it was impossible, was essential, but perhaps his biggest gift was the confidence he always seemed to have in me. I was a real scientist now, and I was loving it.

9

On the Last Field Trip of the Season
Terra Ceia Bay, Florida

As the *Disconnected* putts through the slow, no-wake zone in the bay, I'm reflective. It's almost the end of August and my first field season as a rogue scientist is coming to a close. Now the real work begins: data has to be organized and analyzed, and grant reports have to be compiled to show funders how I've spent their money this past season (to hopefully help them see why it was worth it). Kathy has collected more than ninety samples in Miami and we got about thirty in Tampa. I'm eager to get them shipped off to Kristina and Sora and see the results of their analyses. I'm feeling hopeful—endings are beginnings and beginnings are full of unknowns. At the start of the season, this new life I imagined for myself was an unknown. I had no idea if this way of working would be feasible for me; I just had a hunch that this was what I needed to do—and I had Tonya as my role model to show that it was possible. Now I'll have to figure out if remaining independent can be sustainable for me in the longer term.

It's a perfect day—one of those days that simply makes

you happy: happy you pushed through whatever you pushed through so you can just be here, now, on this beautiful water. It's a little above eighty degrees, with surprisingly low humidity for South Florida, and there's an easy wind. Water is splashing into the boat as the wind picks up, and we bump off the small waves. I smell the crisp scent of salty air.

But then the wind shifts. The pungent odor of rotting fish hits me. I know that smell: it's a red tide bloom. Red tide is caused by a naturally occurring algae, but at a higher-than-normal concentration (or bloom), this algae, *Karenia brevis,* which produces a brevetoxin, a chemical that can damage the nervous system and result in death for fish and other vertebrates, can be harmful. During a red tide bloom, not only are marine animals exposed to this toxin, but the bloom and subsequent die-off of algae also sucks most of the dissolved oxygen out of the water, effectively suffocating anything with gills. A red tide bloom feels apocalyptic the first time you see it: all the dead fish floating on the discolored water, which smells awful. In fact, this phenomenon isn't good for any of us: brevetoxins can be released into the air and cause breathing issues for people, too, as well as other problems for anyone eating the infected fish and shellfish.

Fish kills in the Gulf of Mexico and along the Florida coast have been recorded since the time of the Spanish explorers in the eighteenth century. But historically, red tides happened every few years, maybe, at most. That was until the 1990s, when their frequency began to increase enough that the Florida Fish and Wildlife Conservation Commission (FWC) created a red tide task force. Sadly, since then, the problem has only gotten worse. In the past six years, the red tide blooms have increased to yearly and then to multiple times a year in some parts of Florida. The reason? Rising seawater temperatures are one known trigger, as well as a host of other coordinating factors, like water salinity, pollution, and wind in the area.

Lately, I've been helping Dr. Jayne Gardiner, a colleague and collaborator at New College of Florida, and some colleagues at Mote with a project looking at how large marine predators—like sharks, as well as rays and snook—are responding to the increasing occurrences of red tide in the Gulf. These folks have been working on this project since 2016, during which time there have been several red tide blooms. The investigators have a large amount of data, and they want to figure out how the animals reacted. Did their movements change during red tides? Were they able to seek refuge, and if so, where? They've asked me to help them make sense of this data, using something called network analysis, which can synthesize a lot of location data. Network analysis isn't a typical tool for shark scientists and biologists, but it's another GIS tool I learned from geography classes I took in graduate school, so I applied it innovatively to my sawfish project; and because of my expertise in how to apply geographical tools in ecological contexts, I'm able to be helpful with their study.

Tonya shifts the boat into idle when we come to a spot that she explains was pretty active with fish last week. We set the gill net out and sit. After some time, everyone takes out their lunch. Tonya and I catch up on our thoughts regarding our favorite TV show, *A Million Little Things,* and all the parts that made us cry.

In spite of the red tide and the smell that makes us hold our noses, we agree we've smelled worse; it seems like the bloom may be coming to an end. We're actually enjoying the day so far. *Maybe this is how life goes,* I think. You hold your nose through bad stuff, without letting it interfere with your enjoyment of the good things . . . but the bad may or may not come back with a vengeance.

That afternoon, we catch several cownose rays. With cownose, you never catch just one, as they travel in large schools. They are often the first to return after a red tide bloom, or perhaps they never leave, which is something else we are interested in understanding with our research. We debate going farther out to see if we can catch more, taking our boat beyond the bloom to an area where the red tide count is low. But the weather report says the wind is going to pick up later, and if this happens it will mean going past our personal limit of twenty knots, so we call it an early, easy day.

I put my white-rimmed sunglasses on and settle beside Tonya as she puts the boat in gear. I look around and feel blessed that I have surrounded myself with supportive people, that I was able to rise above and create something beautiful for myself and others. Something that never ceases to amaze me is the way that we Black folks are able to come back from adversity. No matter how many times we are knocked down, we continue to get back up, one way or another. I just wish it didn't have to be so hard. But, like my ancestors before me, I am resilient.

.   .   .

I was still at the College of Charleston when I came as close as I ever want to experiencing an act of terror. It was the early summer after my sophomore year, and I went out with friends to a bar called Fish to watch Colombia play Brazil in the finals of the Copa America. I couldn't care less about soccer, but I was happy to hang out with friends and enjoy an easy evening out. Everyone was chatting, laughing, drinking, and having a good time while the game was on.

After a while, I got up to go to the bathroom and pulled my phone out of my pocket for the first time that evening. I had more than thirty missed calls. They were from my mom and a bunch of friends; weirdly, they all were asking, "Are you okay?"

Yeah, I'm great! I thought. Maybe it's weird that I didn't think something was off about so many missed calls and texts, but I was recently back from a semester abroad in Trujillo, Spain, and figured I had a lot of catching up to do with folks I hadn't seen in months. Plus, I was in such a calm, mellow mood from hanging out with my friends that my mind didn't make the jump that something could be wrong. But then I noticed a Facebook message from my host mom in Spain asking if I was okay. I had *just* seen her and she wasn't the type who would send a message for no reason. Only then did I realize something was truly the matter. I texted my mom. "I'm good. What's up?"

"There's been a shooting in Charleston," she wrote.

My heart sank.

I pulled up Google and learned that there had been a shooting at the Emanuel African Methodist Episcopal

Church. Mother Emanuel, as it is affectionately referred to in the Black community, was *one* block away from where I was standing, on Calhoun Street. I had sung there with the gospel choir just that past fall, on Founders Day.

There was not much other information then, just a few details: a white male in his twenties attended Bible study at the Black church, and after sitting with them for an hour, opened fire and killed nine people before fleeing.

All the ease and all the light of a relaxed summer night was knocked out of me. I left the bathroom and walked over to my friends, who were still laughing, half watching the big screen behind the bar.

"Check your phones," I said.

They pulled out their cells and saw that all of their people were calling and texting them, too.

I looked around the bar, which was filled with almost all Black and brown people, and I could see the slow transfer of information over the next few minutes as people's loved ones contacted them. The mood in the room shifted, became subdued and tense.

"What do we do?" I asked the table. I knew they were thinking what I was thinking, which was that we were in the only bar in the city that tended to attract Black and brown folks. If there was somebody literally around the corner looking to slaughter Black people, we were sitting ducks. One of my friends stood up to leave, but the bouncer stopped him at the door.

"Sorry," he said. "No one is allowed on the street right now. Everyone has to stay inside."

My friend came back to the table, and we just sat there, our eyes on the door.

"Well, on the bright side," Kat said, "if a racist white guy did walk in, he would stick out like a sore thumb."

Later I learned that the man who decided to shoot nine people dead at Mother Emanuel had also stuck out like a sore thumb when he came to Bible study, but they hadn't turned him away. They had welcomed him with love.

"I know that's right," said Tyler, one of the two white people in our group that evening. "If aaaaany other white boy try and roll up, I'm tacklin' him!"

I have no idea how long we sat there, but it felt like several hours. The crowd on the television was excited about something—a goal, perhaps?—but I really didn't care. Finally, they let us go—I don't know why. The killer was still at large as far as I understood, but we were free to walk down the street. And that two-block walk back to campus was the longest of my life. It felt so far. I felt so unsafe, and I had always felt safe in Charleston, which had almost no major crime. Bike theft was the biggest issue around campus.

The next morning, the perpetrator was arrested in North Carolina. Flags were lowered. However, the Confederate flag over the state capitol remained at full mast, while the Stars and Stripes was at half-staff. Per legislation, the Confederate flag was not to be lowered without two-thirds of the vote of the state legislature, and so it stayed put. The stark visual message could not have been louder: We, the people, have no respect or regard for Black life; you can be killed while in prayer, and while we failed to protect you, we will protect this symbol of hate. But it's okay, because we sent our "thoughts and prayers." Every other flag was lowered in mourning, but this one was left to remind me and mine how little we mattered. The flag blowing in the wind, proudly defiant to the pain I was in, was a reminder of the long history of white organized violence against Black people.

I was working in Gavin's lab that summer, and our group was scheduled for a meeting the next day. He emailed everyone to say that if people wanted to be together, we could gather, but it wouldn't be a lab meeting—we would just all be there and could talk. I went. I learned Gavin had been nervous about my whereabouts because I was the only Black student he had. He knew I went to church, but didn't know which one, so he was worried that Mother Emanuel was my church.

Over the following days, more and more details came out about the terrorist and the arrest. On the news, a clip was released of the police walking him to their cruiser, and it was so striking to see. Only a few months before, in Charleston, a Black man was brutally killed during a traffic stop. But this new arrest video was so calm, almost relaxed; clips showed the killer being walked to police transport in a bulletproof vest so no one would assassinate him. I remember thinking, *The people praying in church didn't get vests!* I was so angry.

At a town hall meeting on campus, I learned that one of his potential targets was the Black Student Union at the College of Charleston—in other words, my community. It was the only space on campus, besides gospel choir, where I wasn't one of the only Black people in the room, if not the only one. But the school had key cards and security in some buildings, and so the terrorist figured the church would be easier. The church was welcoming to all, as was made painfully clear by a detail that the killer told investigators: that he had hesitated to go through with the shooting because the churchgoers had been so nice to him. But later, he wrote in his journal, he did not regret what he did, did not regret killing innocent people. He felt it had to be done for the crimes of Black people against white people. Which is an interesting take on U.S. history considering there was a whole period of time when white people enslaved Black folks.

The Confederate flag continued to fly above the state capitol until a thirty-year-old Black woman named Bree Newsome scaled the flagpole with rock-climbing gear and tore it down. After she was arrested, the flag was replaced, but Bree's actions provided another powerful visual, and I was proud of her. One month later, the state legislature officially removed the flag, after fifty-four years of flying it above the capitol. (Perhaps it's worth noting that the flag flying was not, in fact, a longstanding tradition—it had been in that particular spot only since 1961, just as the civil rights movement and integration were taking off. Officially, it was to commemorate the centennial of the Civil War—but I think it was South Carolina's middle finger to Black folks, who were starting to get more rights.)

When I walked by Mother Emanuel on the way to class the following semester, I saw a sea of cards, flowers, and stuffed animals that people had left outside. Although I'd walked by many times before, I finally took in what a beautiful building it was: all white, with a peaked steeple and arched windows. As I stood outside, the air around the building felt heavier.

I found myself taking deep, reflective breaths. A moment of silence and prayer. This building was completed in 1872 after the original church, at another location, was destroyed by a white mob after a failed slave revolt; for years after the attack, the AME congregation in South Carolina was scattered: some went to white Methodist churches where they had limited rights, while others met in private, until a new church was built. This new building, on the site where Emanuel sits today, was then damaged by an earthquake in 1886. The church was rebuilt in 1891 and has been lovingly maintained since then. She is a reminder of the resilience and strength of my people. When I thought about Dylann Roof walking through her doors I was flooded with anger, frustration, and sadness, but I felt further inspired to fight against hate.

The church was only a few blocks from the waterfront, so I decided to walk toward the river, just to sit and look at it, to reflect. Whenever I needed to feel rejuvenated in Charleston, that's where I went. The water would restore me, filling me up with its calm and peace, and when I was fully recharged, I would go back to campus. In the lab, my work on the phylogeny of sharks was waiting for me. Not for the first time, I felt the connection to sharks and amazement at the unlikeliness of their survival. At each mass extinction, they prevailed. After a white mob burned the church to the ground, we rebuilt it. Due to racial hatred and stereotypes, the killer who murdered those people in the church perceived them as somehow threatening to him, even though they were simply gathering to pray. So much of the language that is used around sharks is also the language that colonizers or racists have used about people of African descent—frightening, beady-eyed, even sharp-toothed.

Despite my anxiety and the challenges I faced, including the murderous white terror perpetrated only a block from where I was sitting, I made it to graduation. There were so many factors that contributed to that: the mentorship and the funding I received, my own hard work, the support of my family, and of course the inspiration I drew from the resiliency of sharks and of my ancestors. But, even on my graduation day, there were enduring reminders of hatred and violence that is uniquely anti-Black.

That morning, my friend Cait, who had taken a photography class, was snapping graduation pictures of me near campus.

"Wait," she said suddenly, interrupting her flow of shots. "Turn this way." Only after I repositioned myself did she resume taking photos. "There was a guy marching with a Confederate flag behind you," she said, as we reviewed the pictures on her screen. Believe it or not, the Secessionist Party of South Carolina was still marching through Charleston every Saturday morning with the Confederate flag.

"Really?" I asked. I looked around and saw the guy. "I actually want him in the picture," I said. "Let's get a shot of him at my graduation, of me celebrating my success with that person in the background."

"Really?" Cait said.

"Yeah," I said. "Like, here I am walking out of the College of Charleston with not one, but two degrees, a bachelor of science in marine biology and a bachelor of arts in Spanish; and this loser is walking up and down the street every Saturday morning holding on to a symbol of his own defeat."

We walked down the street in the direction he and a few other people were moving. And then, when they stopped for a moment, she held up the camera.

"Smile," she said.

10

At the Virtual Florida State University Mentorship Training

Now that the field season is over, it's time to plan for the next one. With Kathy taking more of a leadership role in the bonnethead project, I'm not sure what's next for me. More hammerheads, minus bonnets? Sawfish in Tampa? But there is always some drama in the sawfish world: the latest is that they are revoking permits and further limiting who can handle these endangered animals. I want no part of sawfish drama. I had a blast this season, but if I decide to go ahead with my own research, I need to start thinking about what my next project will be and how I'm going to fund it.

But that's an issue for another day. Today I'm running a Diversity, Equity, and Inclusion training for my old biology department at Florida State University. In the last two years, aquariums, university departments, and nonprofits have hired me to offer DEI trainings to their staffs in the hope of preventing the kind of attrition of students and faculty of color that happened to me. Today, I'm facilitating a virtual workshop called "Entering Mentoring" for my alma mater, to facilitate tangible, immediate change for faculty and, in turn, my fish-loving, talented friends in school. I do it for my friend who is criticized and told she doesn't work hard enough because she leaves the lab at 5 p.m., when her adviser doesn't know or care that she must leave because her family has only one car and each of them needs it for work. I do it for my friends who are still in the lab, working hard and trying to protect their mental health, while casually being asked to do menial errands for other members. I do this for the nervous Black students who know they are capable and talented but are surrounded by people who undermine their value to the group.

In my experience, researchers and scientists who believe themselves to be evidence-based people can sometimes have a hard time accepting their biases. This is because they see themselves as rational—and so they can't imagine that they could be biased toward anyone at all. My goal is to provide faculty with a few tangible tools they can use to check themselves for bias and make sure they're not making unfair assumptions. They can take these tools and use them the very next day with students. If I help just one well-intentioned mentor develop allyship skills, perhaps their future mentees will feel supported and will have a better chance to thrive in the lab.

When each attendee comes on my screen for the Entering Mentoring workshop, it's one familiar face after the next. Dr. Dean Grubbs shows up, and I can't suppress a smile. Dean is the head of his own lab at FSU; he was my grad school adviser and remains a friend and mentor. He's a busy guy, and his being here today means he has gone out of his way to do so.

I drop a small note to him in the chat. "Hey Dean."

"Hey!"

Dean probably spends two hundred days a year on the water and endless hours writing grants. He has no Stop or Pause button, just Go all of the time. He's got a bit more silver in his hair than the last time I saw him a few months ago, on a sawfish survey on Tonya's boat, but otherwise he looks like his wily old self. The wily old self that doesn't turn the boat around even when the wind is blowing at over twenty knots, with whitecaps everywhere. This Entering Mentoring session is not a required event for him, since he is not technically part of the biology department, and it means a lot to me that he's taking the time.

I see a few faces I expected to see, such as two faculty from the DEI committee that organized the workshop, including the one person of color on the faculty. I also note that several people who could benefit from this session are not present. Like the chair of the department. Also, *that professor*—I can't even remember her name, but she is tenured and rude, and I had prepared myself for how to respond if she did show up. But she didn't.

I start the session with a review of what the Center for WorkLife Law has named common bias syndromes. We start with "Prove It Again" syndrome, which describes how individuals in groups that are stereotyped as less competent often have to prove themselves over and over—and *over* again—while individuals in groups that are stereotyped as more competent may be judged on perception. Success can be attributed to luck for a marginalized individual, while for others it is attributed to skill; mistakes are noticed more and remembered longer.

After that, I talk about the "Tightrope" syndrome, which

describes when a supervisor unconsciously allows for a narrower range of workplace behavior for women and people of color. For example, they may discourage directness or assertiveness in a Black woman, while encouraging it in a man. And then we finish up talking about the last two: the "Parental Wall," the pattern of bias that affects how people treat parents (and sometimes nonparents) because they are perceived as less dedicated to their work or vulnerable to judgments of them as a parent/person, whether they work too hard or not hard enough in the workplace; and "Tug of War," the pattern of bias that causes infighting among marginalized people due to the perceived scarcity of opportunities in an oppressive workplace.

Once I've gone through all the syndromes, I break the attendees into small groups for an exercise where they create a rubric they can use to ensure they are measuring mentee performance fairly instead of with standards that disadvantage those with less socioeconomic privilege but who are capable of doing the work. First, I have them think of five core traits or skills they are looking for in a mentee and brainstorm all the ways (traditional and nontraditional) that those things could be demonstrated. I also have them list high-impact factors (things that might indicate mentorship would have a greater impact on a particular applicant), like financial barriers, lack of access to resources (like the ocean or research facilities), or being from a historically excluded group.

Next, we look at sample case studies. Each group looks at a real-life situation and talks about what they would do in the situation and why. The first case study we discuss is "Is it okay to ask?" Here, a Black student who was doing well has left the program and the faculty member doesn't know why. The professor has heard through other students that the student was having issues as the only Black person in the lab, and the faculty member wonders if they should ask the student about it.

I drop in and out of the small groups and listen to them talk it out.

"Generally, I think it's okay to ask, but at this point perhaps it's too late," one person offers. "That would be a question to ask the student while they're in the program. Like a check-in."

"The relationship would already need trust," says another. "You couldn't just swoop in."

"If you have a trusted relationship, wouldn't they have told you that these issues were happening?"

"Maybe, but maybe not. Asking them after the fact, though, doesn't help them stay in the program, whereas checking in with them while they are there could potentially help. Also, asking afterward shows that while all of this stuff was happening for the student, the teacher didn't even notice."

Back with the whole group, someone from that breakout shares.

"Only two of us in our group have ever had a Black student in our labs. And, in talking, we realized that neither of us asked [those students] what their experience was like at FSU. Both of our students finished. We had good relationships. But since a former grad student of this very department—*you*—is here talking to FSU faculty about how to do better, that leads us to believe that there is room for improvement in our department."

Another participant agrees. "To ask about race or to ask

someone who is a different race from me how that experience is for them is just something that never occurred to me. It's not something I knew to think about or ask." He pauses, and then says, "But I should have asked. I feel like we had a good enough relationship that they would have told me, but I should have asked. I should have opened the door first."

"As the mentor, yes," I say. "You should ask those questions. If you want to be someone who helps provide a safe space for all the talent in your lab, you will need to know what, if any, invisible or difficult issues students may be navigating. You know what it's like being in this department as a white man. But do you know what it's like in this department for someone who is a woman? Or Black? Or not from this country? Or gay? You can't know unless you ask and then listen."

I drop a few links in the chat about listening skills and preconceptions. There are ways to talk with someone and ask questions about their experiences that could truly offend or hurt them. But there are also ways to invite conversation about race, identity, or lived experiences that signal respectful curiosity rather than ignorance or judgment. Good mentors are hard to find, and while I really enjoyed my time working with Dean, I was glad to see he was there pushing to improve his skills as a mentor and an ally even further. Good teachers and mentors—not one or two every now and again, but across the board—can make a big difference between a student thriving and contributing to science or leaving the field. This loss of young talent is a missed opportunity for all.

.   .   .

I've been fortunate with mentors, and I'll always be grateful to Gavin for many things, including introducing me to Dean. Toward the end of my undergrad career at Charleston, Gavin made me an offer: he was moving to another university and he wanted me to go, too.

"If you want to come with me, I'd be happy to have you," he said. "You can get your PhD. You don't need to do a master's. You've already done master's-level work as an undergrad in my lab. I feel confident you're prepared for PhD-level work."

I was tempted, but I knew in my heart that Gavin's specific area of study wasn't for me. I'd tried out lots of different areas of marine science work to figure out the direction I wanted to go in. I'd done a study of coastal acidification, examining water quality, and volunteered with the Marine Mammal Stranding Network, doing necropsies (which are basically autopsies on animals). I'd looked into microplastics and their effects on the ocean. I was waking up to all the ways that human interaction with the marine environment could be destructive. Gavin's research was lab-based, a lot of working with genetics, pipettes, and computers, but I was really itching to get outside on the boat; I wanted to interact with live animals in the wild, to do applied science with clear policy implications, to try to figure out how to protect precious marine wildlife that was coming increasingly under threat. And I knew I still wanted to work with sharks. What Gavin did in his lab was amazing—but my passions lay elsewhere.

When I explained this to Gavin, he told me, "Well, in that case, you need to meet Dean. That's exactly what he does."

Dean is a fish ecologist and the associate director of research at Florida State University's Coastal and Marine Laboratory. Most of his research addresses conservation issues concerning sharks and rays, with a special focus on smalltooth sawfish, which, as you'll recall, are endangered. Dean was spending his days out in the field, surveying, asking questions. Gavin wrote an overly complimentary and embarrassing introductory email to Dean, in which he said I was one of the best students he'd ever had and that I would be an asset to Dean's lab. Later, Dean told me that Gavin had never written him a letter like that before, and so he immediately said yes to meeting me.

The first time I went down to visit the Grubbs lab in Tallahassee, my dad came with me. Right away, my dad developed a man-crush on Dean, who was a country boy with long hair and a wide, mellow smile. Growing up, Dean told us, he spent his youth fishing and exploring Florida's Gulf Coast. That love of the water and wildlife led to his degrees in marine science and biology, and his PhD in fisheries science. What charmed my dad even more was that Dean lived on a farm with an eclectic mix of animals: a llama, a couple of zebu, ducks, pet raccoons, a pet squirrel that he sang karaoke with, and some fainting goats. He loved to hunt, grew vegetables in his garden, and was pretty much self-sufficient. "If it wasn't for your mother," my dad told me, "this is how I'd live."

Dean explained to me that he didn't have a lot of funding for his graduate students, but said if I was able to figure out some funding on my own, I was his first choice. Both Dean and Gavin helped me write my application for a National Science Foundation Graduate Research Fellowship Program grant. Not long after I submitted my application, I got the news that I'd won it. I had no idea what a big deal this was, until I got to FSU and students came up to me and said, "*Whoa!* You won the GRFP?" Being awarded this fellowship, particularly just coming out of undergrad, is extremely rare. But Gavin and then Dean never seemed to doubt my abilities, and so I never knew to worry; I just did my best, since that is all I can do anyway.

Arriving at Florida State University, however, was daunting. It was a huge university, nothing like the relatively small liberal arts school I had been at. When I pulled into the parking lot in my blue Honda for my first day of graduate school, there were so many people there. Cars were cutting one another off and stalking behind other cars to get a spot when someone pulled out, and I couldn't find a place to park. I had arrived with what I figured was time to spare, but after circling and circling the lot, I was twenty minutes late for class, and still I couldn't find a parking space. I'm a punctual person: I hand papers in on time; I arrive at the time I say I am going to arrive. The fact that I couldn't even figure out how to park my car the first day of grad school threw me off-kilter, when I was already nervous.

I began to feel the familiar heat of panic start in my throat, and the loud beat of my heart in my ears. I could tell a panic attack was about to hijack me, and so before I could black out, I left. I tried to make it back to my house, but the heat was rising too quickly, and I pulled over. On the side of the road, I had a full-blown panic attack. My head got heavy, and my body couldn't tell if it wanted to throw up or go to sleep. I must have been breathing, but I couldn't feel anything but heat rising and tingles sparking all over my legs and my arms. I just sat there in my car, sweating. I'm not sure how long this went on, but as soon as I was able to breathe normally again, I called my mom.

My mom hadn't been doing well lately. We'd known for a while that something was wrong—she was having breathing difficulties, pain in her joints—but no one seemed to know what the problem was. At first the doctors thought it was pneumonia. Because my mom was a veteran, she got care through the VA, but the doctors there couldn't puzzle it out, so we decided to get a second opinion, and then a third. It turned out that Mom had a very rare autoimmune disease that affected the lungs and the joints. Since the day I came into this world, my mom had been my emotional rock, my source of stability and calm. When I was at Charleston, I had been closer to home, about a two-hour drive. Now I was nearly seven hours away from her, and I already missed that closeness like crazy. The change and uncertainty surrounding my mother's health and being so far away from my family wasn't helping as I tried to adjust to this new city, new school, and new responsibilities.

"I don't know what I'm doing," I told her over the phone, still in panic mode. "I can't find a place to park."

My mother's voice calmed me. "Breathe," she said. "Just breathe."

I breathed in through my nose, then slowly out through my mouth, like I was blowing bubbles under water.

"Go home," my mom said. And it felt like permission. "That's the best thing to do. Just go home, calm yourself down. Try again tomorrow. Some days you gotta know when to hold 'em and when to fold 'em. And this is a fold-'em day. Go home."

And so I missed my first day of classes in graduate school.

Back in my new house in Tallahassee, I lay down with the lights off, quietly returning to myself. Where Bruce Banner turns into the Hulk, Jasmin Graham turns into the Husk: all my anxiety, fear, nerves, doubt, insecurity, and overwhelming frustration take over. I'm able to navigate life when I manage the Husk, making her dormant. But then there are times when I can't find a parking spot when it matters most, and she hijacks the car and takes me home midmorning.

The next day, I tried again. I left super early. I got my parking spot. It honestly felt like a major relief. I walked to class on time, as if nothing had happened the day before. But then, within minutes of my first class starting, I thought, *Oh, you are in over your head.* School had always been easy for me. But grad school was entirely different. In grad school, they don't really teach you. They talk at you, and you figure things out on your own. It's very self-directed. I was still expecting faculty to teach me, like they had in college and all other schooling before. But it was clear this was nothing like college.

In some ways, graduate school was exactly what I had hoped: I had access to an amazing adviser and field research opportunities. Dean was on the Smalltooth Sawfish Recovery Implementation Team, which meant his lab went to the Florida Keys, the Everglades, and even the Bahamas on sawfish surveys.

The Everglades is one of the most beautiful places I have ever been. It's miles of undeveloped land; it's the way I imagine the world was before people came in and mucked it all up. You can see all kinds of wildlife, listen to the sounds of nature, and totally disconnect from the rest of the world.

It was in the Everglades that I first met Tonya, who would become such a mentor and inspiration to me. The first day on the boat with her was amazing. She was kind, funny, and made a point to explain everything she thought I might be unfamiliar with. And the best part was . . . she brought crack. No, not the drug—#SayNoToDrugs. "Crack" is what she calls her snack mix. Every day of fieldwork she puts a wide assortment of junk food, including Goldfish, pretzels, Nilla wafers, Teddy Grahams, and Fritos, in a large bowl. Each day's mix is different based on what was on sale at the store, but it's delicious every time. I don't know what it is about putting a bunch of junk food in a bowl that elevates it to the next level, but it's addictive (just like crack).

Baby me holding a baby smalltooth
sawfish in the Everglades

In addition to going out in the field with Dean and the recovery team, I got to join them at their annual meetings and observe their conservation work firsthand. It was exciting to learn about new technology, too. It was Dean who introduced me to the ways that scientists were trying to work together using telemetry networks. The Integrated Tracking of Aquatic Animals in the Gulf of Mexico (iTAG) and Florida Atlantic Coast Telemetry (FACT) were two collaborative networks of scientists who agreed to share their receivers with each other to be able to track animals more effectively. Receivers were expensive, and so even a research program with a lot of money might have only a few in a specific area. Therefore, scientists decided to work together and let one another know when anyone else's animals passed their receiver. Everyone signed a contract stipulating that the data belonged to the one who tagged the animal. I was happy to learn about these networks, because collaboration was the best way I knew to move things forward.

I spent the first year of grad school reading, trying to look for a novel question to ask for my research and thesis project. Because Dean was on the sawfish recovery team, this afforded me great access to sawfish conservation work in Florida. A lot of work had already been done on these charismatic endangered animals, so I began to read up on sawfish habitats, migration patterns, and ecology. I realized that not much was known about the movements of large juveniles and adult sawfish. There had been many studies of these animals as babies—by Tonya and other members of the recovery team—but once they grew to be larger than about two meters long and were big enough to leave the nursery and fend for themselves in open water, we didn't know where they went, what they did, and why. This was a data hole I thought was interesting and that maybe I could fill.

At the time, there were two common methods for animal tracking, both with pros and cons. The older method, which Dean and the recovery team had used for years, employed satellite tags to track the animals. The tag was attached to the animal externally, on the dorsal fin. It could track movement for 60 to 150 days, estimating the animal's position and storing that data in the tag until it popped off and floated to the surface after its designated time was up. Once at the surface, the tag was able to transmit the archived data via satellite, and it is at that point that the researcher has access to all of the data the tag has collected. This satellite tracking wasn't terribly accurate, but there was no limit to its range: it went everywhere the animal went and so the researcher didn't risk losing the animal.

Meanwhile, the second, newer method was more accurate, but more limited in range. A researcher could implant an acoustic transmitter under the animal's skin, so there was no risk of it falling off, and the transmitter sent a signal that pinged nearby receivers. These transmitters lasted for up to ten years and could tell you almost exactly where an animal was; however, they could do this only when they were within range of a receiver. No receiver, no tracking information. So we could track an animal's movement only along a route of receivers. Sharks can traverse entire oceans, so this new tracking technology was exciting for what it offered—yet had very real limitations.

In the end, I figured out a way to combine the best of

both worlds: I started taking data from the satellite tags and pulling acoustic data from the receivers as well. I had a huge amount of data but I wasn't sure how best to synthesize it, until I applied a tool I learned about in a geography course: geographic information systems. This tool helps geographers predict the location of certain weather patterns, among other things, and seemed like a perfect fit for what I was trying to do to potentially predict where sharks would be at certain times. With these creative, unconventional choices in my methodology, I was beginning to find my unique, Jasmin-way of solving problems and being a graduate student. But what came next didn't just throw me off stride. Frankly, it crushed me.

11

At the MISS Regional Meeting
Myrtle Beach, South Carolina

In the space of two years, our organization has grown from four people meeting up on Twitter to more than four hundred members, with people all over the country meeting regularly, both virtually and in person. We've gone from an idea to a force for change. Over the summer, I sent out an email to members in the area inviting them to a regional meeting in Myrtle Beach. This will be a chance for any local MISS members to socialize and get to know one another. We have MISS members all over the country and when we can get folks together outside of Florida, we try our best. Carlee, one of my co-founders, will attend as well. I'm excited: we were able to collaborate with Ripley's Aquarium to host this event, coordinating a behind-the-scenes tour, a shadowing experience with some of the shark husbandry staff, and even a dive in their shark exhibit.

When my dad learns that we're going to be swimming with sharks at Ripley's, he decides that's something he doesn't want to miss, and makes the three-hour drive down from Columbia to watch us.

On my way to the aquarium, I walk past Broadway at the Beach, the kids' paradise I loved growing up. Turning the corner toward the boardwalk, I brace myself to see my old foe the dragon in the volcano. But when I look up, he's gone, and I actually feel a pang of sadness. Almost everything I grew up with has been replaced.

Thankfully, the aquarium is much as it used to be when I was a kid—it's actually celebrating its twenty-fifth anniversary this year. I go in and meet up with Carlee and the other MISS members. It's early in the morning, around seven o'clock. First on the agenda is working with the husbandry team to do a health assessment of their cownose rays. This is a lot of fun for both me and the members because we get to learn how to use an ultrasound machine to scan the rays. Next we prepare for our dive. The goal is to do our frolic in the tank with the sharks before the aquarium opens so there aren't a ton of spectators. We all go to get suited up in our wetsuits, masks, and tanks, and the aquarist gives us our safety instructions. Everyone is excited. When my dad arrives, I pop out to get him from the front of the aquarium, then walk him in and over to the tank. He plants himself in the tunnel that runs underneath the big shark tank. I'm told we will spend the first part of the dive in this area right in front of him.

The first group of divers are already in the pool—four of them—so I stand and watch with my dad. Then I'll go in with Carlee.

"What in the world . . . ?" my dad says. He can't believe his eyes. The aquarist is waving a pool noodle in the face of a big, beautiful, pebble-colored sand tiger shark with its

A sawfish sits on top of the glass tunnel at Ripley's
Aquarium in Myrtle Beach, South Carolina.

signature long, spiky teeth. I love sand tiger sharks because
their teeth make them look like they are desperately in need
of an orthodontist.

"Is she fending off a shark with a pool noodle?" my dad
asks, laughing.

"The sharks aren't going to actually bother anyone," I tell
him. "You just want to let them know which way to go, like
traffic cones. Give them a heads-up. Traffic cones aren't going
to stop you. They just let you know: 'Not this way.'"

Sharks have certain areas that they swim in, their own
paths and patterns. Here, they've been trained to follow the
aquarist's pool noodle instruction—so when she waves it,
they know not to swim there. I think about Genie Clark,
the Shark Lady, who was really the first one to figure out that
sharks could be trained in this way—her techniques are still
used in aquariums, enabling the sharks to swim up and feed
in the same place every day.

"What's up with the sandbars?" my dad asks.

Sandbar sharks are also swimming around in the tank. They're small, slender, brownish creatures and they do not follow the pool noodle thing. They just go wherever they want to go. In fact, no one even bothers to train a sandbar because they're so fast and agile that they tend to curve and move at the last minute. They're also small enough that they don't get in the way—unlike the sand tigers, which are massive. No one bothers to train the sawfish, either, because they just sit. You'd have to push a sawfish to get it to move. And then it'll move only slightly, clearly thinking: *Am I out of the way now? 'Cause I just wanna lay here.*

Finally it's my turn to dive. I leave Dad in the tunnel and go up to the edge of the tank. I step into the water by the sea turtle feeding area, which is shallow. The green sea turtle eats here separately because she's a bully and likes to steal the sharks' food (even though she is a vegetarian). She goes into her feeding zone and eats while the sand tigers are getting their lunch. Now she paddles over to me, hoping she'll get something from me, all *Hello? Do you have some food for me?*

"No," I tell her. "I don't have anything for you, I'm just here."

She quickly decides Carlee and I are boring and leaves.

I wade in a bit deeper and then dunk under the water. Right off, I get a great view. I can see the whole tank. There are colorful reef fish and large groupers circling about. I dive deeper until I'm on the inside of the glass spectator's tunnel. Then I go over to the feeding spot where the sawfish like to hang out. As I swim, I stay as low as I can to the bottom: you can't surface in the tank because it confuses the sand tigers.

They're sensitive and skittish, and when you disrupt what they are used to, they freak out. One of the aquarists told me about the time she fell into the tank by accident, and all of the sand tigers swam away and wouldn't come to the surface for days. Honestly, they sound more skittish than Iggy.

Carlee Jackson Bohannon and I explore the
bottom of the tank at Ripley's Aquarium as
a sand tiger shark swims overhead.

We stay in the tank for nearly an hour. I spend most of the time looking through the sand under the feeding station, collecting shark teeth. I even find a piece of a chipped sawfish tooth, which is very exciting. I have a moment to commune with a sawfish who comes over to say hello. Even the sea turtle passes by to pay us a visit. It's really cool to be inside the same tank that I spent most of my childhood looking in at through the glass. By the time we are wrapping up, the aquarium has opened, and I see the faces of small children smooshed up against the glass, staring at us. *Huh,* I think to myself. *Is this what it feels like to be a fish in an aquarium?*

While we are diving in the shark tank at Ripley's Aquarium, I take a moment to "high-five" a MISS member through the tank glass.

My dad has left by the time I climb out of the pool, off to visit other friends and family members. I change out of my wetsuit, and we have our MISS meeting in the aquarium conference room. The aquarium staff have provided us with a lunch, and several of them come in to do a career panel discussion. The regional meeting goes great, and as all the members leave, we promise to keep them posted on when we plan on having another one in the area.

After the meeting is over, I call my dad.

"All done?" he asks.

"Yep, just finished," I reply.

"Let's meet at Aunt Rose's house; we can leave your car there."

After that, we get in his car and drive around the piers, looking for places to put up Tonya's sawfish signs. Sawfish seem to be moving farther and farther north, along with their mangrove habitats, and so I'm hoping to talk to people who are fishing to let them know to be on the lookout for them, and to contact us if they see anything.

We don't need to use Google maps; we just go by my dad's memories of the piers he used to fish at and where his friends go. The first pier we visit is the one where he and I used to fish the most, back when I was a little kid. I feel a wave of nostalgia start to wash over me and then I see the sign: $5 ENTRANCE FEE; $10 IF YOU WANT TO FISH.

What the heck? I remember watching my grandma fish here! And in all those years hanging out with my dad, never once did we have to pay!

There's a teenager standing by the sign, collecting money.

"Hi," I say, and introduce myself. "I'm a scientist, and I wanted to see if I can talk to the person in charge?"

"The pier is owned by somebody," the kid says, shrugging, "but I don't know who. I just collect."

"Is there someone I can call?"

He shrugs again.

"Here's my card," I say to the kid. "Maybe you can give it to someone who could call me. I'd love to ask them questions about the pier."

He nods and we go.

Our next stop is Cherry Grove, another favorite fishing

spot for my dad. But the pier is blocked off. It's not clear why. There's caution tape barring the entrance and a NO TRESPASSING sign. Another pier nearby looks like you need to go through a restaurant to get to it, so it's probably also private.

Onward to the next pier.

"There used to be one right here," Dad says, but we're just looking at a plot of nothing, a few broken planks so busted up it seems *possible* a pier was there once, but now it's just junk.

"Hurricane must have got it," he says.

And we go on. Nearly every single pier we remember is now private, and someone is charging to use it, or it's just gone. And at the ones that remain, where they are collecting money, the people using them are white. Where have all the Black fishermen gone?

The pier at the state park is the only one where we actually pay and go in. This is the same place where civil rights protesters tried to integrate the beach sixty years earlier.

The guy who owns the bait shop next to the pier collects the fee.

My dad says, "I'm a senior. So I'm at least free, right?"

"No."

"Man, I've been waiting sixty years for that senior discount!" My grandmother used to love fishing here back in the day because it was less crowded since it cost money (and was the only fishing pier back then that did), but seniors didn't have to pay. Not anymore.

There are a few people fishing. As with the private piers, there aren't any other Black people here. It's an all-white crowd.

My dad chats with a guy who is fishing with two poles. Dad recognizes the setup, because he also fishes for king mackerel a lot and knows that you use one line, which is anchored to the ground, that keeps the fish from swimming too far away, then cast out with your second line, which gets close-pinned to the anchored line.

"Hey, man. Catching anything?"

"Eh, few things," the guys says. His wife is sitting next to him, and she smiles.

They get to talking, because my dad will talk to anyone and everyone.

"This is my daughter. She's a scientist," he says, introducing me.

"Oh, very cool," the guy replies.

We learn the guy is not from South Carolina, but he and his wife moved to Myrtle Beach a few years ago and enjoy the fishing.

"Have you seen any sawfish around here?" I ask.

The man shakes his head. But he does confirm that he knows what they are and what they look like, so that's good. I give him a flyer.

With a nod at one or two other folks fishing, we return to the car. When I was a kid, this pier would be full of thirty or so fishermen at any given time, with coolers for bait, snacks, and drinks. Most of them would have looked like me and recognized my dad from the neighborhood. But as we walk back down the pier, no one calls out to my dad in recognition. If folks aren't fishing here anymore, where are they fishing? They have to be somewhere.

The questions swirl in my brain. Could this be the new project I've been waiting for?

.   .   .

At FSU, the initial phase of my sawfish thesis project was going really well: I had won a prestigious grant to fund my work, and I was uncovering new information about where these critically endangered animals spent their time. I was collecting a lot of data, and I had identified a great way to determine not just what areas these fish were using but also how high the rate of bycatch might be for them in those important areas.

On board the *Disconnected,* downloading data from an acoustic receiver

Then, one day, Dean got an email from a fellow researcher who has been and shall forever be known in these pages as Dr. Minion (my therapist in graduate school suggested that if I ever had to interact with him, I think of him as a minion from *Despicable Me,* to keep myself from curb-stomping him). Minion said that he'd like to write a paper about the presence of sawfish on his receiver and asked if he could have the metadata for these animals that he had picked up on his receivers. On his own, Minion could only see the tag numbers each time they pinged on his receiver, but he couldn't access details about the animals they were attached to, such as size, sex, and maturity. As is customary, he offered us co-authorship on his study, and we declined. Dean told him that these data were part of a larger study that I was doing and Minion had only a small part of the picture (information just from his receiver). As such, Dean could see that Minion was potentially exaggerating the importance of the region where his receivers were. Minion said he wouldn't use the data, and we thought that was the end of that.

But, in the new year, Minion wrote again to Dean to say that he had other sawfish data, not just mine, so the animals for which he was requesting the metadata were in fact part of a larger study he was doing. Now, if he had a full study going on, which my material would fill out some, that would be collaboration, and collaboration is essential to science. But Minion was not a sawfish researcher, and did not have a permit to handle sawfish, and so it was unclear how he would, suddenly, have significant sawfish data and research under way. Not if he was following the proper research guidelines laid out by NOAA, the federal scientific and regulatory agency. Dean once again declined to share the metadata, now suspicious of Minion's methods and ethics. We *hoped* that was the end of that.

A few weeks later, though, Dean and I got an unhinged email from someone at NOAA whom neither of us knew, decrying our lack of scientific collaboration, a core principle in advancing science, and telling us that we must turn over our metadata to Minion. Phrases were in bold; exclamation marks were plentiful; nonsensical half sentences screamed outrage at our lack of scientific ethics and our selfishness. NOAA is a funding source for much of Dean's research, and so the email effectively bullied Dean into turning over our metadata. He replied to the email in a much more calm and reasonable way than I could ever have mustered. He also copied this man's boss and boss's boss, in hopes that someone else at NOAA might step in to address the unprofessional behavior. However, we never got any further response from this crazy guy at NOAA or the higher-ups. I was shocked that nothing had been done about this man and his very unprofessional and threatening email, but it seems to me that in the science world, people—especially older men—get a lot of free passes. NOAA also didn't look into Minion, who claimed to have sawfish data yet did not have a sawfish permit; they appeared to be taking a path of no effort. The telemetry networks also didn't hold Minion accountable for violating the agreement we had all signed not to claim data from animals other scientists had tagged. Instead, he remained a member in good standing and they let him take my data and use it to make inaccurate claims about the area around his receiver.

Minion was also a member of the American Elasmobranch Society, but when I tried to get action taken within that organization, I was told the code of conduct covered only what occurred at conferences or during official AES-sponsored events. Unethical scientific behavior was, therefore, out of their jurisdiction, and Minion could indeed remain a member in good standing with them as well.

Minion's behavior was one thing, but the failure by the larger scientific community to take appropriate action was even more frustrating to me. It felt like an affront to my work and everything I stood for. I believed someone was stealing from me, but no one in power seemed to want to do anything about it.

Why was no one doing the right thing? The harder thing, but the right thing? Why was Minion allowed to get away with this, without any consequences for his career? And what was the point of someone like me doing so much hard work if it could be stripped away at any point? I wondered if this would even be happening to me if I were a white male.

At the annual sawfish recovery team meeting later that year, at Dean's suggestion, I pitched the team to pool all their sawfish data into one larger synthesis paper that would look at the large-scale movements of smalltooth sawfish; I would lead the synthesis paper and use it for a chapter of my master's thesis. This would give me a really robust dataset to work with. The random slice of data that Minion had would pale in comparison. Everyone agreed to go ahead with this plan.

Their decision should have made me happy. And I *was* honored to be the lead on a big study. But the events with Minion and, even more so, the lack of consequence for his repeated behavior, were taking their toll. I was struggling. There were big personalities in the sawfish group, and we were trying to work quickly so that our paper would come out first, before Minion's. I was so stressed my hair began to fall out. Over the next few weeks, I burned out completely.

For two months after my research was essentially stolen, I fell into a deep, deep hopelessness. I stopped everything. Each morning, just to move and pull myself out of bed seemed to require more energy than I had or was able to give. Getting dressed was too much: too much for my brain and for my body. So except to walk Iggy and go to the store, I stayed in bed. I didn't go to the lab. I didn't see my friends. It's not that I didn't see the point, or that I was feeling "down"—it was more than that; I was trapped in a huge, endless, blank space of nothing. I was devoid of all impulse, just a body with a dog to take care of, so I walked him, and I fed us from time to time. When I am low, I usually go to the water, but I didn't even do that. No water, no science, no support, no future, no lab work. Science had always been fun for me: it was what I was good at and what I enjoyed. It was the place where I got to fully be all the things that made me *me*—curious, playful, brave, detailed, focused. But now it hurt more than it was fun. Nothing was fun. Nothing filled me up, and I had nothing left to give.

My mom was still sick at the time, and as much as I didn't want to burden her, she was the one who always knew what was going on with me. She was worried, and suggested I make an appointment with a free therapist through school. The therapist put me on medication and eventually referred me to group therapy. Slowly, the combination of the medication and going to the group helped me to feel the first glimmer of my old self. A small one.

There were other grad students from different departments at the group therapy meetings, but I didn't know any of them. That anonymity and sense of community helped. They had endured awful, awful things—some that I couldn't even imagine. We'd sit and listen to one another. So many people, all going through so much grief. And in this circle of grieving people, we decided—or I decided, with their support—that I had to go. Leave academia. Leave FSU. That I needed to remove myself from a world that could treat people the way it had treated me. I had given the best of myself to science, and the institutions within my field had allowed Minion to take my work, ignoring the impacts this would have on me, my work, and even the species they claimed to want to protect. Worse: they supported him. *They* put the rules in place to protect ethics within the field, but they didn't care enough to apply those rules for me. Yes, I had the potential to do big things, huge things, even, but not if my bucket was being emptied out over and over again. I needed people and things to fill me up, too. If I was only giving and other people were only taking, I couldn't keep doing it. I needed to be in places with give-and-take; otherwise, I couldn't continue, even if I wanted to. And the thing was, I didn't want to.

One evening, after a day in the field in the Keys, I walked up to Dean as he was sitting on a picnic bench outside and told him quite matter-of-factly, "I'm done. I'm leaving FSU in December with or without my degree." He didn't argue; he just assured me that he was going to get me to the finish line in December and I would be walking out with a degree. I feel Dean supported me in the best way he knew how, but it was not enough; it was time to go.

From the outside, it might have looked surprising. I was leading a huge team of scientists on a paper that was uncovering new and really important information about a critically endangered species. Even if and when Minion published his work, my work would be far more impactful. Not one sawfish researcher supported Minion's research, and I had the whole team on mine. So why not just keep going, stay the course? Push through? I felt like I was back at the Spring Valley magnet program all over again, where I knew I needed to quit if I was going to survive high school at all. Back then, people asked, "Why would you leave this prestigious program that helps people get into the top colleges?" To which I might have replied, "Well, for one, those top colleges aren't designed for me, either." My Duke "acceptance" didn't account for the generations of wealth that had been stolen from my family members as they attempted to be self-sufficient business owners, only to be beaten back at each chance by anti-Black forces determined to keep them down, leading to the generational poverty my parents worked hard to claw their way out of, but which still didn't result in a savings account large enough to cover Duke's tuition. But more to the point, or more central to me, was that the environment and culture at Spring Valley had left me hollowed out—the things that I loved, the things that brought me joy and filled me up, had gotten swallowed in the madness. And the same was true for academia and science.

I had kept in touch with Tonya since the first time I met her in the Everglades with Dean, and I continued to view her as a role model. So I started looking for jobs in the Tampa area, where she was, so I could be in her orbit. I spoke Spanish, so I thought perhaps I could look for translation work, or do bilingual education somewhere. Anything but science. I eventually found a job at Mote—not doing science but coordinating a project for the intern program addressing racial inequity in marine science. It surprised me how well this job fit. In that position I would have the chance to make a science space easier for someone like me. I was out of the field already, I told myself, but maybe I could help keep others from experiencing some of the difficulties I'd had to endure.

Before starting work, I went home for a month. A month of rest. My parents instinctively knew to leave me be, so it was a quiet, calm time. And I slowly became myself again and felt ready to start my new life in Tampa. Then, a few short months later, the pandemic hit, and it was like the world pressed Pause, just like I had. Working from home, I continued to recuperate.

While Iggy and I kept each other company, I watched the news like everyone else, as a modern-day lynching was broadcast all over the internet. After George Floyd, there was increased awareness about Breonna Taylor, Ahmaud Arbery, and many more Black people murdered without legal consequence. Growing up Black in America you understand this reality, but for many in white America, free from distractions during the "Great Pause," something shook loose in them for the first time. It was as if people around the country finally realized Black Lives really *did* Matter. While white America was having this great awakening, Black folks were thinking, *Welcome to reality. Where y'all been at?*

It was while scrolling, scrolling, scrolling one day through #BlackInNature and seeing so much joy and calm that I came across Carlee's picture. And, as they say, the rest is history. Connecting with Carlee, Amani, and Jaida and creating MISS, having people from around the country and then the world join us, and then being on the water again with Catherine and the people at the Field School, doing science with them on the *Garvin* . . . something clicked into place.

The claws came out—I wasn't going to let them get away with it. The journal that eventually published my paper also published Dr. Minion's, and they published him first. If you read our papers side by side, you'll see that mine is more robust and refutes what his said. To make this explicit, I added a piece in my paper specifically to address his false claims. In doing so, I unfortunately had to give him a citation (which is like currency in the academic world), but it was worth it.

I also filed a complaint with his university. I knew from experience that the university probably wouldn't do anything. So I gave them a year to actually respond to my complaint with real action or recourse of some kind; otherwise, I told them, I would take my complaint public.

Over the next year, as MISS continued to grow, I increasingly felt like I didn't need to wait for these weak people in academia—who may have had "power" but were too scared to use it, too concerned about their academic careers or the fallout—to do anything. I realized I actually had an advantage over those people: I no longer had to worry about my academic career, because I had dropped out! So I was like, *F*** it! I am not afraid. I am holding you useless, selfish people accountable, even if I go down, whatever the consequences.* I was willing to go kamikaze if it meant taking the system down with me. And when I flipped that switch in my brain from being worried about my career to not being worried, I realized that I *did* have power. Not only could I take myself out of a harmful situation, but I could hold people accountable, simply by letting them know *I* was not having it. Because if I was going to be ostracized and mistreated by the science community regardless of whether or not I did what I was "supposed" to do, I might as well make a frickin' scene. And if my actions could keep someone else from experiencing what I had, then it would be worth it.

It was fascinating to notice that once the switch flipped in my brain from feeling powerless to empowered, people actually became intimidated by me. It's really hard to control someone once they realize that *they* have power, after all.

12

At the AES Conference
Spokane, Washington

Five years after my first unfortunate experience at an AES conference, and two years after I left academia, our small but mighty group of MISS members rolls up together to Spokane, Washington, for this year's AES conference. There are eleven of us all together, as well as several Friends of MISS (FOM), people who don't identify as gender minorities of color, but who have joined the MISS network to support our MISSion and act as allies. This is going to be a very different experience from that first meeting I attended in 2017—where I was one of only two members of color and where there was a fight about whether or not to introduce a code of conduct. Coming to the conference is really a test run for us: Can we make it a positive experience for our members, or do we need to leave and try another society?

I haven't even gotten to my hotel room before a mentee of mine comes to find me in the lobby. I know she has been worried about seeing an old adviser—who is an AES member—but she tells me she is feeling relieved, sort of.

"He's not here, but some of his students are."

"Let me know if you have any problems," I tell her.

I feel like a mama bear, ready to battle anyone who is tryna mess with MISS folks.

I see another MISS member arrive, and I greet her. It's the woman whom I met at that AES meeting years ago. She waves and looks genuinely relieved to see me. I haven't missed an AES meeting since that first one, but she hasn't been back since then. Yet when she heard that a bunch of MISS members were going to this year's conference, she said she would give it another try.

"Hey," I say with a smile.

"Heeey," she replies with a mischievous grin of her own. "You ready to get voted onto the board?"

That's right—during this conference's business meeting, the election results will be announced. If I get voted on, that will help tip the scales so that the board is no longer just a *majority* of people interested in change, but a *supermajority* big enough to make change actually happen. If I get elected, I will be able to help prioritize making the membership more diverse and improving the overall quality of the society.

"Honestly, give me strength if I do get elected," I say.

"You'll always be my president," she says, making me blush.

"Did you get your MISS guidebook?" I ask her, holding up our pamphlet, along with some of the other MISS swag we're giving out.

I made a booklet for members as a complementary guide to the conference at large, with contact info for MISS and Friends of MISS attendees, and a schedule of presentations by our members and friends highlighted among the four full days of events, talks, and socials. In the past, I've found lunch to be the most awkward time, so, like I did in middle school, I decided to make a new table. My booklet has a list of MISS members and Friends of MISS who are serving as lunch buddies each day for anyone who wants to eat together, the same way other people at the conference all seem to do with one another. At the bottom of the last page, I made sure to include an important note: "If you have any issues or concerns, please contact Jasmin Graham." I've also included the way to signal if you find yourself in distress or need someone to come help you get out of a situation.

MISS members and Friends of MISS at the 2022
Joint Meeting of Ichthyologists and Herpetologists

MISS members are given a blue MISS lanyard to hold their conference badge, while the Friends of MISS are given a gray lanyard so any MISS member can glance around a room or an audience during their talk and easily spot MISS folks. Each year, several audience members seem to try to give presenters, usually women and early-career folks, a hard time with questions that are designed to make them look stupid. Several of the MISS members have expressed concerns to me about the presence of these people at the conference and fears about entering the space. In my experience, such fears are completely warranted.

On the first official day of events, I give my talk on ally skills. Without any funding for our DEI initiatives yet (our grant proposal is out, and we may or may not get funding from that next year), I decided I would still run a session during the conference, not a mandatory paid training for leadership, but an offering to anyone interested. Of course, it is scheduled in conflict with another event, so it's a small but mighty showing.

On the second day, a person who has been worried about drama at the conference is indeed cornered and harassed by her former adviser's students, and I go into full-mama-bear mode. I tell her to report what's happened to the conference safety officer. She is hesitant, and I understand her fear of retaliation, which had already happened once to her, so I let her know she only has to do what she truly prefers. No matter what, I tell her, I will *personally* ensure something is done.

"You are not here alone," I explain to her. "We have your back the whole way."

She decides to report the situation, and the safety officer reports it to the conference administration, but all the while, the people who cornered her are walking around like nothing has happened. Later that day, she is supposed to give her first-ever scientific talk at a conference. Giving a talk to fellow colleagues is nerve-racking, and I don't want her to have to experience something going wrong because of these other students in the audience. So when I arrive in the auditorium for her talk, I take matters into my own hands. I text her, *What are they wearing? Where are they sitting?*

She lets me know. I locate them, somewhat toward the front, though not front and center. I slide into their row, taking a seat right beside them. Then I stare directly at them. Just stare. One of them gives me a look out of the corner of his eye. I don't say a word, but my eyes are speaking volumes: *I see you. I know what you did. Try something. I dare you.*

All I hear is my blood pulsing through my ears. I want nothing to spoil this moment for her. Just before the Q and A, the bullies leave, and I take a deep breath and exhale. Seems like I legitimately scared the daylights out of them, but I want them to know that *someone* is watching; there is *some* accountability for them trying to harass or intimidate people.

"I think that went really well," I say to her after the talk. "Nice job out there."

"Thanks," she responds. Then she adds, "What did you say to them?"

"Nothing," I reply, and laugh. "I didn't say a thing."

For the rest of the conference, the students don't bother her; they won't even make eye contact or even be in the same room with her. They leave her entirely alone.

.　　.　　.

At the business meeting the next day, I have no role. I am just there to listen. And there is a lot to hear. The MISS members flood the board with questions about how the society might support them. Then it comes time for them to announce the election results and the new board members.

"Jasmin Graham!" my good friend Tonya reads my name.

I have been elected to the AES board for six years. Okay. The room erupts into applause. There are the MISS students, just hollering and smiling, so proud of *me.* One of AES's major funders is there and he is applauding, too. I see friends, like Miki and Lisa and others who have been working to change the makeup of the board for years, smiling broadly. It is such a big moment for so many people, as well as for me, and, if I'm being honest, even though I am nervous, I am also touched. The day I stopped worrying about my career and started operating on a principle of pushing for change, I thought there was a very good chance I might be torpedoing many of my professional relationships. But sitting in this room full of MISS and AES members applauding my election to the board, it seems that my "f***-it" approach to holding people in high places accountable has resulted in the opposite response. I've just been embraced within my field, elected to the board of the American Elasmobranch Society. My loyalty to myself and my community, it seems, is also my power.

The last night is the banquet. This is the same banquet where, in the past, female members reported being groped and otherwise demeaned. Tonight, I am the DJ, taking requests all night long. Everyone from the MISS group is dancing. The woman who swore she'd never return to AES tells me she had a great time at the conference. So in the end, our experiment to see if we can insulate MISS members at the conference succeeded, with only one person having a challenging incident.

As an organization, AES is trying to get better, and there are so many people here working hard to make it a place that supports all of its members. The biggest roadblock I see is not the shrinking faction of older members who actively resist change, but the majority of members who won't get into the fray, who don't support our efforts to actively make change. What's true of AES is true of America at large. Whether the problem is racism, sexism, or the destruction of the natural world, inaction can be just as harmful as negative action. Doing nothing, by default, supports the status quo.

13

A Postseason Lunch and Meetups
Tampa and Miami, Florida

"Dr. Minion is out."

I freeze. My burger is midair and my mouth is open. I'm speechless. I've just returned to Tampa, where I'm having lunch at the Salty Dog with a colleague. After a few months in South Carolina with my family, I knew I was out of the loop a bit, but wow.

"The announcement hasn't been made yet," my colleague tells me. "But he is resigning."

My thoughts fly all over the place:

Hallelujah.

Why the heck did it take so long?

Is this real? I'll believe it when I see it.

And on a Friday afternoon later in the fall—when this type of email tends to go out, burying the story as people head out for the weekend—it's official. The university announces Dr. Minion has resigned, and that his replacement is none other than Dr. Catherine Macdonald. *Did I read that correctly?* Catherine?! Literally, the original Friend of MISS? A scientist who supports all students, including women and people of color, is now the head of what was once one of the most toxic labs in shark science?! I have many chances to read the email because screenshots were forwarded to me from friends, colleagues, and MISS members around the shark world many, many times.

I text Catherine: "Congratulations!"

She replies: ☺

A few weeks later, we Zoom so I can congratulate her face-to-face—and also talk about next steps for me. The fieldwork for the bonnethead project is over. I'm helping my colleagues with the project they are doing on the increased occurrences of red tide, but really, I'm in the midst of trying to figure out where I want to go next in terms of my research. If I want to do more field research projects, then I need to figure out my own boat situation. My science shed is finally finished, and the types of questions I plan on asking will determine what equipment I buy—should I beef up my science shed into a super-shed, or should I invest in a boat?

"You could always go back to graduate school," Catherine says, smiling. "You know I'd love to have you."

I am flattered, but unsure. In so many ways the offer is attractive. It's a coveted program, and it's now going to be run by someone I trust completely to support me and anyone getting treated unfairly. I would be able to reenter the doctorate track, and maybe even end up as an HBCU professor with her own lab, like I used to dream about. We also both know that without a PhD there are real limitations to funding, too, because some important agencies that fund a lot of work hardly ever fund a researcher without a PhD—looking at you, National Science Foundation.

"It's one good way to get access to a boat," Catherine says, but she can tell I'm not biting.

"I'll definitely think about it, but you know I hate Miami, right?" I say. "The people there are extra. For no good reason! And don't even get me started about the traffic."

We both laugh, but I'm joking only a little. The truth is, I don't want to go back to graduate school. When I was at FSU, I had Dean in my corner, and it wasn't enough. One or two allies aren't sufficient when a whole system needs to change. Now there's Catherine, and it feels like the tides are starting to change and we are moving in a truly positive direction. This is a victory through and through. But I finished my first season as a rogue scientist, and I had a blast. I helped give so many people opportunities they never would have had before. In taking stock of the situation, I realize this: I'm happy in Tampa, and this happiness is hard-won. I'm committed to running MISS and being a support system to whomever needs me, while still doing research independently and staying rogue. I have plenty of folks in my corner, and although I don't benefit from the money and infrastructure of an institution, I've learned over the past year that there's always a workaround—I can leverage community resources, collaborate, and use plain old duct-tape-and-zip-tie-style innovation. Necessity is the mother of all invention, after all. My mental health and my joy right now is more important to me than putting myself in another environment where I might be prone to the Husk taking over, with her anxiety and panic attacks.

"Keep it in mind," Catherine tells me.

And then we talk about what might come next. I tell her

about the idea I had after being back home recently to collect local ecological knowledge from Black fishermen in Myrtle Beach. My dad knows people who have been fishing their spots for half a century or more, almost every single day. They have so much knowledge of the fishing stock and patterns, but no one ever talks to them to learn what they know. Plus, I'm so curious about where the heck they are now, since that walk with my dad revealed that the piers and a lot of the places they used to fish have become privatized. I know they still have their places. They always find places. Catherine says that another co-founder of the Field School might be able to help with crafting questions for informal but structured interviews. She suggests that we approach the inquiry from a social-science as well as ecological lens. She really likes the idea, in part because it's totally different from what anyone else we know is doing. In talking with her, I start to feel really excited about the potential here.

"How's Kathy doing?" Catherine asks, moving on to the bonnethead project. Technically, Catherine is Kathy's adviser, but I have been doing the mentoring on this specific project. I give her the update: the morphology of the bonnetheads in Biscayne Bay versus Tampa Bay appears to show that the females in Tampa tend to be bigger than the ones in Biscayne. She didn't find a statistical difference though.

The results from Sora's lab so far show that the bonnetheads in different locations are eating different things, and so this seems like the most likely explanation for their differences, but of course we need more data to make a determination. The analysis of their genetics should be coming soon. But the most interesting and curious thing to come out of this is that as they get older, the male bonnetheads' heads get rounder, or less pointy. You see, the general thinking is that bonnetheads, like humans, start out looking similar in some ways, and become more different as they mature: just as human males grow taller and their voices drop during puberty, sexual dimorphism often becomes more apparent with age due to changes in hormones as animals mature. Scientists expected this sexual dimorphism in head shape to work similarly in the bonnetheads. The study that first identified sexual dimorphism in head shape hypothesized that baby bonnetheads start with rounder heads no matter the sex, but as males mature their heads get pointier, while female heads stay round. But that's not what Kathy found: her data is showing that the males start pointier and get rounder, and that males and females appear different as babies and start looking more similar with maturity. I cannot for the life of me understand why this would be. As is so often the case in science, you go looking for the answer to one question and end up with another unanswered question altogether.

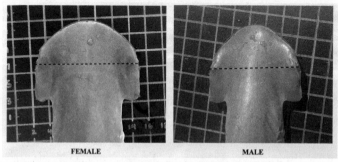

FEMALE   MALE

Screenshots showing the differences in head shape
between male and female bonnetheads

196

I tell Catherine that we did not discover a new species of bonnethead. Dang it. But I still want to figure out what the heck is going on with them. Suddenly, my next independent field season is taking shape, and I start doing the rogue-scientist math: How do I get myself a boat when I don't have boat money?

After the call with Catherine, I immediately type out a list of the different equipment I would need if I want to start my own field setup, not one reliant on the Field School or Tonya's schedule. My own boat, equipment, gear. I text Tonya, "Can I go shopping for field gear in your garage?" I figure I could pull together a bunch of stuff from Tonya—she's got tons of old gill nets, longlines, floats, and so on that she isn't using—and write a grant for whatever additional gear I'll need to buy. She replies right away: "You know it!"

I also need a boat. But buying my own is just too expensive. So over the next few weeks, I do some research and decide to join a boat club Tonya told me about once. Membership in the Freedom Boat Club would be a lot cheaper than buying a boat, but it would offer me access to a fleet of vessels to choose from whenever I need to go out on the water. I pay an upfront membership fee and then can check out whichever boat I want whenever I want. So when I need to do offshore stuff, I can take an offshore boat, and when I do inshore stuff, I can sign out an inshore boat. Over the winter, I'll write grants to set myself up for the next field season with access to a boat and my own gear.

Days like this help me realize that there's so much power in doing what I enjoy when I'm healthy and whole. I'm able to do big things for others when I feel this way, because doing for others is what I love. Protecting sawfish, bonnetheads, MISS members, my parents, my friends: this fills me up. But I can't give if my bucket is empty, and my bucket empties fast when I work too hard in environments where I'm not totally respected, appreciated, and understood. Who, really, can stay healthy and whole in such an environment? It's amazing to know that Catherine and a growing number of allies I work with every day are among the ones making decisions now. It's beautiful to know that I have all sorts of options, traditional and nontraditional, for my career, and that through my work as a rogue scientist and with MISS, I have helped create choices for myself. But for now, Tampa is where I am most able to be full and whole. Black, proud, nervous, and nerdy. And so I choose me, so I can be strong for the marine life and communities who need me the most.

Epilogue

Postseason, November
Myrtle Beach, South Carolina

"What do you think, Daddy?" I ask my dad at the dinner table on a visit to my parent's house. "Wanna help me with a science project?"

I want to see if he can help me find people to interview for my project collecting local ecological knowledge from Black fishers—men and women like the ones who used to fish with my dad. I want to find out *where* they are and *what* they know. So many of my dad's friends used to fish every day, for years, so it seems to me they must know a thing or two about marine life. And yet they are never usually involved or included in the conversation. Fishermen—particularly fishermen of color—are often regarded in conservation circles as uneducated and lacking in knowledge. It's assumed that only the researchers and conservationists themselves can see the bigger picture. But there is value in this local ecological knowledge, I'm sure of it.

My dad looks at me like I've just asked him to do the most exciting thing a man could ever dream of doing.

"Of course!" he replies. "I know people we can talk to!"

"You can be an author on the article, too," I say.

He waves me off. "I don't need to be an author."

"Well, Daddy, by academic standards, if you contribute, you should be credited as an author."

My dad says he can take or leave the credit—he just wants to spend time with me—so he agrees.

We set aside a day to drive around together, with a handful of questions drafted by another co-author on this project, the social scientist from the Field School whom Catherine mentioned, Julia Wester. The first person we want to talk with is my cousin, who loves to fish. We call ahead. He doesn't answer his phone. But he never answers his phone, so my dad and I drive over to his place anyway and knock. When we pull up to his trailer, we see my cousin has a mean dog out front.

"No way I'm getting out," my dad says. I respect that.

He tries my cousin's number again, because he's probably there, but he still doesn't pick up, so we move on to the next person on our list.

In conservation circles, protecting fish is often framed as environmentalists versus fishermen. Catch-and-release rules and protection zones are created to protect the fish, and fishermen—not just the commercial outfits but individuals out fishing for leisure or for food and subsistence—are blamed for not adhering to these protections and for the decrease in the fish populations. Although this may be true in some individual cases, it's always struck me as out of step with the way my family and community operate. We have always depended on the ocean for sustenance, to put food on the table, so it follows that it would be in our best interest to protect fish populations, not to deplete them.

Although my cousin isn't available, fortunately, my dad's friend *is* home. He's an older man, in his seventies. We sit across from him, and I put my phone in between us to record our conversation. I ask him how many years he's been fishing, and he tells me, "Probably fifty years."

Although fishing was never his main occupation, when he was still working, he would get off the night shift at six in the morning and would be out fishing by six-thirty. Then he'd fish until noon or one.

"When did you sleep?" I ask him.

"From one to five," he replies.

"Oh, goodness," I tell him. "That's dedication."

"It was. I'm telling you . . . I love to fish."

.   .   .

After that interview, we speak to two other fishermen my dad knows. Even in a single day, I learn a lot. Beach renourishment is one topic all the guys bring up. That's when an agency comes in with new sand and replaces, say, ten inches of beach where it has become eroded. Often property owners are concerned about their homes and businesses losing value due to the erosion. All the fishers I interview for my project say the same thing: the new sand harms the fish communities because when a storm comes, it washes away, and then the washed-away sand covers up all the habitats that attract the fish. So not only does almost all the sand that was dumped on the beach immediately disappear into the ocean anyway, but it negatively impacts the marine environment. Why, then, do people continue to see beach renourishment as a solution to changing habitats? Because they're talking only to property owners. They're not talking to the people who are relying on the fish population for food. And so they do not have a full understanding of the cost-benefit of beach renourishment. If the U.S. Army Corps of Engineers talked to the fishermen, maybe they would make different choices. But they don't talk to them. And so the marine environment and those who rely on it suffer. These are solvable problems, but you have to listen to everyone in order to arrive at truly effective solutions. To me, this is the perfect example of how everyone benefits when *all* the stakeholders are given a seat and a voice at the table, not just the people with more money.

Once we finish our interviews for the day, it's still light out, and we're getting hungry. When I'm in Myrtle Beach, my aunt Carol's is the place to go for dinner, so my dad calls my cousin Nina.

"Hey, is Carol making anything for dinner?"

"Whatchu think, Uncle Sidney," Nina says, like, *We have to eat, don't we?* And so we waste no time driving over, because that's as good an invitation as we need to eat with family.

Aunt Carol's is a white house, wood; it has a porch with two little iron pillars—I swear old Black Southern people's houses all have the same porch with the same chipping white paint and plastic storm door. Aunt Carol steps onto her porch to greet us as we pull up. I bet she's been watching from behind the storm door since we got off the phone. She likes to watch *everything* and everyone—without having to contend with the bugs while sitting on the front porch.

We walk up, and my dad blurts out, "What'd you make me?"

Aunt Carol snorts and gives him a dirty look.

"I made something for Jasmin!" She pretends to box him out of the doorway and lead me in. "Come on in, Jasmin. You can come in, but your daddy needs to stay outside."

For as long as I've been alive, my aunt Ernestine has been telling my dad and Aunt Carol, "Y'all need to stop," when it comes to their goofing around and trash-talking, but it hasn't happened yet. My dad and Aunt Carol give each other a big hug. She's maybe twenty years older than him and my dad doesn't see his sisters as often as they see one another, but my dad and all his siblings remain close.

Inside it smells like potpourri and Bengay: another Black Southern old person thing. The house also smells like Aunt Carol's been cooking. And I am ready. While Nina sets the table, my dad, Aunt Carol, and I make ourselves comfy in the living room. She's got two couches, a coffee table, and her little TV. And a recliner that my uncle Baba used to sit in before he passed. That was *his* seat.

The house is open-concept, which doesn't mean anything when on the Hill, other than it's small and there are very few walls. There's a four-seater dining table in one part. The decorating style: throw as many family pictures as possible up on the wall. My mother is becoming increasing fond of this style as well (maybe it's another old Black Southern lady thing). There is a china cabinet with random knickknacks—

Aunt Carol, like most old Black Southern women I know, loves her knickknacks. Little African figurines, figurines of children and dogs playing, souvenir bells. Why do all old Black Southern women have a china cabinet? I don't know, but they do.

Go past the dining table, you're in the kitchen. Past that is the door that goes out onto the back porch, where all of the junk lives, along with the extra fridge. There's the inside fridge and there's the outside fridge. It's a thing. The outside fridge is usually where the beer goes. Or, in my dad's case, all of the things my mother doesn't want to see, like his dead animals from hunts (and also his Blue Bell ice cream; he likes to keep that hidden away outside, too). Aunt Carol is the only person who had inside pets while I was growing up. Family dogs were outside dogs. So everyone gave Aunt Carol a hard time about her inside dogs. But she loved her little dogs and they lived with her until they were old and blind, though they are gone now. She has a little dog figurine under her TV in memoriam.

"So what were y'all doin'?" Nina asks my dad.

"Jasmin is interviewing people about fishing." My dad beams.

"About fishing?" Aunt Carol asks.

"Yeah, I'm going to be published on a scientific paper with Jazz!" he exclaims loudly.

"Oh lawd." Aunt Carol lets out a laugh, ready to talk some trash, I'm sure, but Nina beats her to the punch.

"Sidney ain't never wrote a paper in his life!" she lets out with a cackle. Aunt Carol joins in. It's an ongoing joke in my family that my dad was not super great in school. But school and learning are two very different things. Rich white kids get to have curiosity; poor Black kids do not—the goal seems to be to just move them through high school by getting them to answer the test the way the test makers want in order to get a diploma. And my dad wouldn't follow that narrow, constricting path. An educational system that spits out rather than cultivates a thinker like my dad is useless, in my opinion. The man is one of the smartest people I know: he loves to do and learn new things.

Aunt Carol has made pigs' feet and rice for dinner. It's so good. Aunt Carol can throw down in the kitchen.

Before it gets too late, my dad starts to get up to leave. When my dad says goodbye to his family, it's a multistage process. "Well," he says, "we should get ready . . ." But then he gets to talking, and we do this for about a half hour, until finally I hear him say, "Take it easy."

It's been a good day. Projects like these—that are close to my roots and my heart—are what drive me. This is my

Me and my dad enjoying a day at the beach

reason to stay rogue, without the stability of a position at a large institution—so that I can practice science that inspires me. Here, my curiosity can shine a light on the lives of the marine animals and communities I love, helping to get everyone included in the conversation—not just those who have letters after their name or who own beachfront property.

On our way out of the Hill, we swing by Aunt Ernestine's, because you can't go to one aunt's house and not the others if they are in town. (Aunt Rose is out of town this time, so we skip her house.) We drive past the duplex my dad built in Harlem on that small patch of family land.

"Still here," he says.

"Still here," I say.

Acknowledgments

I'd like to thank everyone who contributed to this book with stories, fact checking, research. I'd especially like to thank Makeba Rasin, who helped me add some serious razzle-dazzle to this book. I would like to thank my publisher, Lisa Lucas, and editor, Anna Kaufman, for believing in this book and not being afraid to publish a book about two seemingly unrelated things: sharks and social justice. I want to thank my literary agent, Chad Luibl, who reminded me that if we all waited until we were old to write a book, we'd miss out on some great perspectives.

Also, a big thank-you to everyone at Pantheon for helping to make this book everything I hoped it could be and more, including production editor Nora Reichard, amazing copy editor Amy Edelman, proofreaders Melissa Pierson and Chuck Thompson, super-talented cover designer Perry De La Vega, and interior designer Mike Collica. Thank you to the marketing and publicity folks Bianca Ducasse, Rose Cronin-Jackman, and Juliane Pautrot.

Illustration Credits

4 Carlee Jackson Bohannon

6 Carlee Jackson Bohannon

13 Courtesy of the Field School

14 Courtesy of the Field School

20 Courtesy of the Field School

29 Sidney Graham

31 Sidney Graham

36 Graham family

40 Courtesy of the Field School

41 Jasmin Graham

44 Kathy Liu

45 Courtesy of the Field School

46 Courtesy of the Field School

47 Jasmin Graham

48 Jasmin Graham

57 Courtesy of the Field School

61 Graham family

66 Courtesy of the Field School

67 Kathy Liu

70 Courtesy of the Field School

73 Courtesy of the Field School

74 Courtesy of the Field School

78 Courtesy of the Field School

84 Jasmin Graham

102 Courtesy of the Field School

114 Tonya Wiley / Havenworth Coastal Conservation

118 Tonya Wiley / Havenworth Coastal Conservation

119 Chelle Blais

162 Jasmin Graham

168 Minorities in Shark Sciences

170 Minorities in Shark Sciences

171 Minorities in Shark Sciences

175 Tonya Wiley / Havenworth Coastal Conservation

187 Minorities in Shark Sciences

196 Kathy Liu

205 Graham family

A NOTE ABOUT THE AUTHOR

JASMIN GRAHAM is a marine biologist in the field of elasmobranch ecology and evolution, currently specializing in smalltooth sawfish and hammerhead sharks. She is a co-founder of Minorities in Shark Sciences (MISS), an organization providing support for gender minorities of color in the field of shark biology and ecology in order to foster greater diversity in marine science. She is a recipient of the WWF Conservation Leadership Award, the Safina Launchpad Center Fellowship, and a National Science Foundation Graduate Research Fellowship, and is the host of PBS's *Sharks Unknown with Jasmin Graham.*

A NOTE ABOUT THE TYPE

This book was set in Adobe Garamond. Designed for the Adobe Corporation by Robert Slimbach, the fonts are based on types first cut by Claude Garamond (ca. 1480–1561).

Composed by North Market Street Graphics,
Lancaster, Pennsylvania

Printed and bound by Berryville Graphics,
Berryville, Virginia

Designed by Michael Collica